D1447676

Sites of Confinement:

Prisons, Punishment and Detention

WITHDRAWN

Edited by:
Victoria Canning

The European Group for the Study of Deviance and Social Control

2014

LIVERPOOL JMU LIBRARY

3 1111 01513 0584

Published by the European Group for the Study of Deviance and Social Control, Weston-Super-Mare, England

www.europeangroup.org/

© The European Group for the Study of Deviance and Social Control, 2014

ISBN 978-0-9511708-6-1

All authors' royalties are being donated by the editor to the European Group for the Study of Deviance and Social Control

The European Group for the Study of Deviance and Social Control held its first conference in Italy in 1973. Since then, annual conferences have been held at different venues throughout Europe with academics, researchers, activists and practitioners in criminology and related fields participating. While initially class and certain political hierarchies were the focus, the European Group gradually sought to address other national, linguistic, class, ethnic, sexual, and gender barriers in an effort to develop a critical, emancipatory, and innovative criminology. This was to be done through the topics of members' research and in the conduct of conferences, with the ultimate aim being to provide a forum for, and recognition of, emancipatory science and emancipatory politics as legitimate areas of study and activism. One goal of the group has been to highlight social problems in the field of deviance and social control which are under-exposed by criminologists in many other contexts; thus to create a forum not commonly provided at other conferences and international networks for academics, practitioners, and activists working towards the promotion of social justice, human rights and democratic accountability.

Dedication

This book is dedicated to Fozia Hanif and Nawaz Khan.

The Contents of this book are based on *Sites of Confinement* Conference held March 2013 and facilitated by the Centre for the Study of Crime, Criminalisation and Social Exclusion, Liverpool John Moores University

Acknowledgements:

Many thanks to the Centre for the Study of Crime, Criminalisation and Social Exclusion for funding the *Sites of Confinement* conference on which this is based. Thanks also to John Moore who handled the production and publication of this book on behalf of the European Group, to Andy Douglas for proof reading, and to all the authors for their contributions.

Note on UKBA

Chapters Four and Five refer to the United Kingdom Border Agency. Please note that the UKBA has since been dissolved and absorbed back into the Home Office. We have chosen to use the original term based on the contemporary nature of the research findings in the chapters concerned.

Front cover photograph:
Border Area of Nicosia, Cyprus by
Victoria Canning

Author Biographies

Emma Bell is a Senior Lecturer in British Studies at the Université de Savoie Mont Blanc. She is author of Criminal Justice and Neoliberalism (2011) and the current coordinator of the European Group for the Study of Deviance and Social Control.

Monish Bhatia is a Lecturer in Criminology at Abertay University, Dundee. His research interests revolve around the areas of immigration and asylum controls, state and corporate crimes and sociology of emotions. Monish has recently been awarded a grant from Carnigie Trust and is currently working on the "destitution and drugs" project.

Victoria Canning is a Senior Lecturer in Criminology at Liverpool John Moores University. She researches the impacts of sexual violence on women seeking asylum, and works with Merseyside Women's Movement, RASA and Migrant Artists Mutual Aid.

Eloise Cockcroft is a Social Worker with Revive in the North West of England, a voluntary organisation supporting refugees, people seeking asylum and other vulnerable migrants.

Vickie Cooper is a Senior Lecturer at Liverpool John Moores University. Her research interests revolve around homelessness and resettlement, including policy responses to the links between resettlement support, homelessness and imprisonment.

Andrew M. Jefferson is Senior Researcher at DIGNITY - Danish Institute Against Torture specialising in the study of non-western prisons and prison reform processes

David Scott is a Senior Lecturer in Criminology at Liverpool John Moores University. David is a former coordinator of the European Group for the Study of Deviance and Social Control and a founding editor of their new journal (first issue to be published in 2016).

Joe Sim is Professor of Criminology at Liverpool John Moores University. He has written a number of texts on prisons from an abolitionist position including Punishment and Prisons (Sage, 2009). He is also a trustee of the charity INQUEST.

CONTENTS:

INTRODUCTION

Victoria Canning

It was during the 2012 Annual Conference for the *European Group for the Study of Deviance and Social Control* that the idea to hold a conference based on confinement came into fruition. A mixture of perspectives at the table asked a number of questions, some new and others long grappled with in Critical Criminology; what does confinement actually *mean*? Is it limited to physical and institutional confinement, or can it be temporal or psychological? Did we all agree on abolitionist perspectives? For those voicing them, what of punishment or deterrence for violent offenders and perpetrators of sexual violence?

As is often the case in academia and activism, the discussion did not end that evening. While consensus was not necessarily met in relation to the questions above, some agreements were made without hesitation. We shared collective concern for the rate of and capacity for confinement, and the exponential increase thereof across many global regions. We unanimously agreed that the introduction of and/or increase in 'superprisons' in a number of countries and jurisdictions has come at the cost of the rights of prisoners and their families. We each recognised that, even beyond the question of violent offenders, strategies in new punitiveness have encouraged mass incarceration, mostly comprised of people from economically powerless or marginalised social backgrounds. As this collection reflects, recognition of the problems inherent in the criminalisation of immigrants, irregular migrants and refused refugees was integral to our debates. We each attested that the incarceration of individuals and families in so-called 'Immigration Removal Centres' has been to the detriment of the values of freedom and civil liberties and stands in contradiction to human rights discourses.

In 2013, at least 10.2 million people were being held in penal institutions across the world (Walmsley, 2013). In relation to this expansion, the rate of incarceration of asylum seekers, immigrants and migrants has exploded across Europe, mirroring and being mirrored by other areas across the globe including Australasia, North Africa and North America (see Aas, 2007). In the United Kingdom alone, space to hold people in Immigration Removal Centres increased from 250 in 1993 to 3,275 in 2014 (Girma et al., 2014). The global outsourcing and privatisation of prisons, probation and detention (to give but a few examples) realises Nils Christie's vision of crime control as an industry (2000). The role of the neoliberal prison shifts further to financial gain and supposedly measurable outcomes of 'reform and rehabilitation'.

This collection of short essays, all based on original research findings, reflects the subject order and content of the European Group for the Study of Deviance and Social Control's first *Sites of Confinement* conference. As is often the case in Criminology, diversity in perspectives can leave some areas of disjuncture, but now is the time to further our discussions and debates around neoliberalism, punitiveness and the challenges of mass incarceration to human, migrant and prisoners' rights. In an era of increased surveillance, control and punishment, how, why and when we challenge the widening nets of penality is increasingly the concern of all of us working in the critical social sciences and criminal justice. To refer back to concerns raised by Stanley Cohen in 1985:

> *When punishment leaves the domain of more or less everyday perception and enters into abstract consciousness, it does not become less effective. But its effectiveness arises from its inevitability, not its horrific theatrical intensity* (Cohen, 1985: 25).

As the authors of the following essays go on to demonstrate in their own ways, the widening net of criminal justice and prison-like controls reaches deep into probation, semi-penal housing facilities and asylum and immigration systems, including mental health support. As Joe Sim points out (this volume), the expansion of the penal to the cultural allows whole social groups to be publicly scrutinised as deviant or problematic, leaving the actions of some (predominantly poor) classes under constant scrutiny whilst the powerful's own (sometimes criminal) actions often go unchallenged. Emma Bell highlights these concerns most astutely through her analysis of neoliberal punitive policy, facilitating a critical analysis of penality that is directly or indirectly inherent in the whole collection.

Order of this collection

As is suggested in the title, there are three key themes to this collection: imprisonment, punishment and detention. It begins with an overview of contemporary neoliberal penal policy, before moving through forms of punishment and control. While the focus lies predominately with the United Kingdom throughout, the policies and political backdrop are not unfamiliar to wider socio-political contexts, particularly in relation to imprisonment generally and immigration detention specifically.

In Chapter One, Emma Bell establishes the contemporary landscape of neoliberalism in relation to its political fluidity and penal dominance. In addressing the development of the expansion of penal policy in this context, Bell argues that the state has not been rolled back as a result of privatisation and welfare cuts, as is often argued, but rolled forward in a way that intensifies securitisation and punishment, presented as necessary to the maintenance of control and social order.

Chapters Two and Three shift to outline specific research projects related to incarcerated individuals and the detrimental impacts of confinement. Vickie Cooper provides an overview of her research in the North West of England which focuses on women's experience of community punishment. Drawing on the issue of risk management, she argues that gendered geographies of dispersal remain problematic for women leaving prison, reiterating wider arguments that women continue to be treated as 'in danger and dangerous'. In the following chapter, Andrew Jefferson summarises a number of ongoing research projects with the Danish Institute Against Torture involving prisons in the Philippines. Through in-depth interviews, he not only draws out detainees' experiences of incarceration, but also the relationships and political or religious beliefs that drive individual resistance and survival across Leftist and Muslim people imprisoned as opponents of the state.

Chapters Four and Five focus on the effects of asylum and immigration detention. In Chapter Four, Monish Bhatia sets the political background of immigration detention in the United Kingdom and addresses the issue of violence and abuse by privately sourced security guards. Based on research into the criminalisation of asylum seekers in the North of England, Bhatia considers ways in which people seeking asylum can be harmed by the system that is set up to support applicants, particularly in terms of detention and incarceration. Through the lens of a case study, resistance to criminalisation is unpacked, providing insight to ways in which the state and private actors can respond when challenged by 'non-citizens', and the problems this can entail. In Chapter Five, Eloise Cockcroft develops similar arguments by unpacking the impacts of asylum detention and criminalisation on individuals deemed as 'vulnerable'. Through her work with Revive UK, Cockcroft facilitates an analysis of ways in which the asylum system compounds trauma for people seeking asylum who live with mental health problems.

Finally, the collection ends with an outline of some of the most significant limitations of imprisonment as punishment. Echoing Emma Bell's arguments at the outset, in Chapter Six Joe Sim looks to ways in which austerity measures have provided an opportunity to increase social controls and further implement penal policy. Sim's penultimate chapter deconstructs perspectives of abolitionism before focussing on ways in which forms of punishment have insidiously facilitated reform agendas which span across and beyond criminal justice. Using contemporary examples, he looks to representations of, and treatment toward, the poor as parasitic and feckless, thus maintaining the populist and punitive focus on crimes of the powerless. In Chapter Seven David Scott moves from analysing the harms of punishment to considering ways in which social control and the widening net of Criminal Justice can be challenged. It is in this final chapter that the basis of the rationale for a manifesto of resistance is more thoroughly discussed, providing the backbone of the aims and objectives of the Prisons, Punishment and Detention Working Group.

References

Aas K.F. (2007) *Globalisation & Crime* London: Sage

Christie, N. (2000) *Crime Control as Industry: Towards Gulags, Western Style* London: Routledge

Cohen, S. (1985) *Visions of Social Control: Crime, Punishment and Classification* Cambridge: Polity Press

Girma, M., Radice, S., Tsangarides, N. and Walter, N. (2014), *Detained: Women Asylum Seekers Locked Up in the UK.* London: Women for Refugee Women.

Walmsley, R. (2013) *World Prison Population List.* International Centre for Prison Studies

6   SITES OF CONFINEMENT

CHAPTER 1:
The Confines of Neoliberalism

Emma Bell

Neoliberalism is a term which is widely used but rarely adequately defined. It is often incorrectly associated with a rolling back of the state yet, in practice, it has actually led to a rolling forward of the state, transforming it in many important ways which have led it to become increasingly authoritarian. Whilst not leading directly to increased punitiveness in the penal sphere, neoliberalism has created the conditions in which carceral expansion becomes more likely as a response to social and crime problems.

Unlike so many other 'isms', neoliberalism cannot be identified with a particular political party, with a fixed geographical area or with a particular person. It has been adopted and adapted in various different ways by seemingly diverse political parties across a variety of states and at different times. Furthermore, it is riddled with internal contradictions. As Hall has said, the term 'is not a satisfactory one', yet it does have 'enough common features to warrant giving it a provisional conceptual identity, provided this is understood as a first approximation' (Hall, 2011: 10). It is 'politically necessary' to do so, argues Hall. Indeed, if we regard this as a trend worth resisting, it is important to name it in order to give it shape and form and thus provide an identifiable target.

Contrary to what is commonly thought, neoliberalism is not anti-state, or at least not in practice. Whilst neoliberals hold that the state should refrain from limiting economic freedom via interventionist policies, arguing that economic freedom is the precondition for personal and political freedom (see, for example, Caldwell, 2007: 67), most do tend to see a key function for the state. Even Adam Smith, often invoked by contemporary neoliberals to give philosophical legitimation to their policies, held that the state should provide the legal framework and the commercial infrastructure necessary to ensure the proper functioning of the market. Hayek also rejected total laissez-faire, highlighting the important role for the state in upholding the rule of law without which freedom would be meaningless (Hayek, 1960). Only the most radical neoliberals, such as Milton Friedman, suggest complete laissez-faire and argue that there is no state function which should be immune to the winds of privatisation.

It was Gamble who coined the term, 'the free economy and the strong state' (1994), to sum up the idea that rolling back the state in the economic sphere led to it being rolled forward in other spheres, thus suggesting that neoliberalism actually led to a certain strengthening of the state. Even in the economic field, the state has not been rolled back. Indeed, Harcourt has highlighted the 'illusion of free markets', arguing that 'our contemporary markets are shot through with layers of overlapping governmental supervision, of exchange rules and regulations, of federal and state criminal oversight, of policing and self-policing, and self-regulatory mechanisms' (2011: 17). Most recently, we have witnessed states across the globe resorting to extremely interventionist measures in order to save the financial sector from disaster.

The state has certainly not been rolled back in the social sphere, even if it has drastically cut public services and sought to limit public spending via a plethora of austerity measures. If we take the UK as an example, whilst many government departments have been subject to significant spending cuts in real terms – with spending on health and education for example down by 5.7% and 0.9% respectively since 2010-11 – overall spending on benefits has actually increased (Guardian datablog, 2012). Furthermore, the state has become increasingly interventionist in the social sphere, most notably under New Labour, as intrusive welfare-based programmes sought to address the social dislocations resulting from neoliberal policies using increasingly coercive methods.

The political need to manage the social fallout from neoliberal policies has made it impossible for the state to disengage from the social sphere, no matter how much it might attempt to dismantle the welfare state. Yet, it has also extended its authoritarian arm in an attempt to deal with social problems by means other than through the welfare state. These two policies are not, however, distinct but very often complementary as social interventions are increasingly backed up by criminal sanctions.

Rather than the state being rolled back, it has in reality been transformed. Instead of intervening in the market and society more generally in order to protect its citizens from the vicissitudes of the capitalist system, it now concentrates essentially on intervening to place the market at the service of the economic elites by opening it up to private interests. Importantly, the neoliberal state has moved beyond *government* whereby power is exercised by the state alone, to *governance*, whereby the state now governs in collaboration with a whole new variety of actors from the world of business and finance (Harvey, 2007:76-7). It would be a mistake to think that neoliberal governance opposes the state and the private sectors. The two are not diametrically opposed but rather flipsides of the same coin. As John Comaroff points out, private enterprise has not replaced the state. Instead, the state itself has become a business, the primary aim of which is to encourage the accumulation of wealth (2011: 145). It is no longer the limit to the market, as the neoliberals feared and social democrats hoped, but is now an integral part of the market itself. Consequently, the role of the state has in no way been diminished. It is of fundamental importance to understand this if we hope to grasp how exactly neoliberalism functions and how it impacts upon the penal sphere.

Aside from economic policies such as privatisation, financial and labour deregulation, and the limitation of redistributive fiscal policies, 'actually existing' neoliberalism was also a social and cultural project designed to instill a competitive and individualistic (entrepreneurial as Thatcher would have said) culture across society by pursuing a deliberate strategy of inequality and attempting to remoralise society. For Thatcher, this entailed breaking from the dependency culture; for Blair it was all about 'playing by the rules' and instilling respect; for Cameron it is about challenging the values of the 'broken society'. Such policies are deliberately divisive, serving to unite the 'respectable majority' behind the neoliberal project.

Rallying popular support behind a project that works against the best interests of the vast majority of the population is indeed the main challenge faced by neoliberal governments. This is where penal policy comes in – it is one way of helping the state to tackle the legitimacy crisis of neoliberal capitalism, never more so than in the wake of the financial crisis. Penal policy is not, as Wacquant argues (2009), intrinsic to the neoliberal project itself but it may be used as a strategy of political legitimation, allowing the government to tackle the social fallout from neoliberal policies. Policy aims not so much at controlling the poor as Wacquant suggests – indeed, they are particularly ineffective at doing so – but even more at rallying the rest of society around the neoliberal project by constructing them as a suitable enemy and scapegoat for the social fallout of neoliberal policies. Punishing the poor, whether by penal or welfare sanctions, is above all politically necessary. Whereas the state has renounced its role as provider of social security, it has reasserted its power as guarantor of the social order. As Hallsworth and Lea argue, the welfare state is being replaced by the security state, characterised by the authoritarian management of the marginalised and socially excluded. Rather than attempting to address social problems via welfare, the security state reconstructs these problems and those who suffer from them as risks to be managed via coercion (Hallsworth and Lea, 2011: 141-4).

Drake has also highlighted the new obsession with security, arguing that it is ideologies of security which have now obtained hegemonic power, encouraging the use of prison and a heightened stress on control within prisons (Drake, 2012). It is perhaps rather ironic that the rise of neoliberalism has been accompanied by the rise of a security discourse which tends, as Drake points out, towards totalitarian tendencies (think of the effective suspension of the rule of law in the context of the war on terror). Yet, in government discourse, it is security which is meant to provide liberty: by neutralising the risk of a few, the safety of the many is meant to be guaranteed. Perhaps the most important effect of the rise of the security state is that of dehumanising those targeted by such measures by presenting them as risks to be neutralised, not as individuals to be helped (ibid: 116). Furthermore, the discourse of security leads to the marginalisation of other discourses such as welfarist ideologies (ibid: 117). Politically, this again helps to legitimise the neoliberal project, shoring up the power of neoliberal governments. It also enables the state to serve its private partners in governance, propping up the burgeoning security industry. Indeed, the current coalition government in the UK has increased the involvement of the private sector in the prison estate to an extent not witnessed since its nationalisation back in 1877. The long-term strategy is that the state will only be responsible for the management of the most high-risk offenders, the large majority of offenders being monitored by the private sector which seeks to gain massive profits from its involvement. The state as a business is now using the delivery of punishment as yet another way of favouring the accumulation of wealth via the free market. Yet, the government presents such a move as being in the best interests of the general public in terms of unproven cost savings. Simultaneously, it presents itself as guarantor of physical security by massively extending the confinement of the poor and the marginalised who become suitable scapegoats for the catastrophic social consequences of neoliberalism.

References

Caldwell, B. (ed.) (2007) *The Road to Serfdom: The Definitive Edition, F.A. Hayek* Chicago: University of Chicago Press.

Comaroff, J. (2011) 'The End of Neoliberalism?: What Is Left of the Left', *Annals of the American Academy of Political and Social Science* 637: 141-147.

Drake, D. (2012) *Prisons, Punishment and the Pursuit of Security,* Basingstoke and New York: Palgrave Macmillan.

Gamble, A. (1994) *The Free Economy and the Strong State,* London: Macmillan.

Guardian Datablog (2012) *Government spending by department, 2011-12.* Available at http://www.guardian.co.uk/news/datablog/2012/dec/04/government-spending-department-2011-12 (last accessed 26 February 2013).

Hall, S. (2011) 'The Neoliberal Revolution', *Soundings* 48: 9-28.

Hallsworth, S. and Lea, J. (2011) 'Reconstructing Leviathan: Emerging contours of the security state', *Theoretical Criminology* Vol.15: 141-157.

Harcourt, B. (2011) *The Illusion of Free Markets: Punishment and the Myth of Natural Order* Harvard: Harvard University Press.

Harvey, D. (2007) *A Brief History of Neoliberalism*, 2[nd]edn Oxford and New York: Oxford University Press.

Hayek, F. von (1960), *The Constitution of Liberty* Chicago: University of Chicago Press.

Wacquant, L. (2009) *Punishing the Poor: The Neoliberal Governance of Social Insecurity* Durham, NC.: Duke University Press.

CHAPTER 2:
Gendered Geographies of Punishment

Vickie Cooper

This essay is concerned with women's experience of community punishment and their dispersal across England and Wales and separating them from their home communities. In this essay I use the concept of 'penal pathways' to broadly describe my record of women's frequent and cyclical journey through prison, semi-penal hostels[1] and their home communities. This essay is based upon an empirical study involving semi-structured interviews with eight women living in semi-penal hostels.

Dispersing Risk out of Area

> *Of all the new actors playing the role of the penal state, perhaps the most prominent is the 'community'* (Haney 2010, p.97)

Currently there are 12 prisons for women, compared with 107 for men (Prison Reform Trust, 2014) and 6 probation approved hostels for women, compared to 94 for men (Ministry of Justice, 2012). There are no prisons or probation hostels for women in Wales and no probation approved hostels for women in London (Prison Reform Trust, 2014; CJJI 2011). Until 2005, there were 28 mixed-sex probation approved premises. However, following a series of inspections of those hostels, the Criminal Justice Joint Inspection (CJJI, (2008) concluded that mixed-sex hostels 'should be converted to single-sex establishments with immediate effect' (ibid:15). Consequently, 26 mixed-sex hostels were converted to male-only establishments, but only two converted to female-only. This differential outcome had

---

[1] The term 'semi-penal hostel' describes the extent to which residents in community-based hostels are subject to both formal and informal strategies of control and describes the way in which hostels are 'not fully custodial or penal in the formal sense', but not 'truly community-based either' (Barton 2005:36).

the immediate effect of scaling down the female probationary estate, leaving only 6 probation hostels for women, compared to 94 for men, with no probation approved hostels for women in Wales or London (CJJI, 2011). This shrinkage of women's probationary estate has resulted in a 'geographically patchy' spread of accommodation for women in the community (Gelsthorpe et al, 2007:51) and, moreover, according to the Equal Opportunity Act 2010 also implies that women are unlawfully discriminated against by virtue of the sex (Barton and Cooper, 2012).

While these structural inadequacies discussed above go some way to explain women's dispersal, they do not alone explain the gendered phenomenon of dispersing women who offend. Closer inspection of risk management for women who offend highlights how 'risk' is measured in tandem with the community environment that led to women offending in the first place. In a report entitled *Local Opportunities*, the Ministry of Justice (2011) explored ways in which to offer local community solutions for women who are deemed to be 'very/high risk of harm' by criminal justice agencies (V/HROH:3) because, the Ministry of Justice concedes, too many women serving a community penalty and/or probation license are sent to hostel accommodation 'out of area' (ibid: 3).

The key rationale for this form of penal displacement is that some women should be removed from the community circumstances that co-created their offending behaviour in the first place; and locating them in a different geographical area will, therefore, increase their chances of rehabilitation (ibid). The underlying assumption of sending women who offend out of area is that women who are V/HROH cannot be sufficiently supported in their home community, not because of a lack of community resources *per se*, but because they may relapse and reoffend.

Closer inspection of assessments that ascertain women's category of risk indicate that women who present acute vulnerability resulting from sexual or partner violence, show that those vulnerabilities are reappropriated and categorised as 'high risk'. According to the Ministry of Justice (2011), the combination of trauma and chaotic lifestyles amongst women in the criminal justice system, coupled with 'compliance issues', has 'led to an inflated assessment of risk by the OM [Offender Manager]' (Ibid:13). The distorting effect of assessing women 'as at risk' of offending or harm, is further compounded by the problem that some criminal justice agency staff 'are inexperienced in working with women' which has also 'led staff to perceived the risk posed by the women as higher than one might otherwise expect" (Ibid:3).

Women's 'risk' in the criminal justice system is therefore often presented as a *fait accompli*, shaped by a crude blurring of boundaries between 'need' and 'risk', where women are deemed to be 'in danger' and 'dangerous' at the same time" (Barton, 2005:42; see also, Hannah Moffatt, 2006).

The Study

This study draws upon a detailed analysis of eight women's experiences of living in a probation hostel and homeless hostel. All female participants have a history of homelessness and imprisonment. For purposes of confidentiality, the city, regional area and hostels where this study was carried out remain anonymous throughout this paper and pseudonyms are provided instead for female participants and the area where this study was carried out. The pseudonym 'Westhampton' is provided as the name of the city and 'host area' (Ministry of Justice 2011:14) where women in this study were sent to and Westhampton homeless hostel and Westhampton probation hostel are the names of the hostels they were accommodated in at the point of being interviewed. For purposes of accuracy, however, the geographical locations where women originate from, as well as prisons and hostel locations that they were previously sent to, are all identified.

Dispersal: Time, Distance and Frequency

The women in the sample included in this study were, on average, dispersed 52.4 miles away from their home community while serving both a community order and period in custody. This distance is probably not out of line with the general experience of women beyond the sample and is actually very close to analyses carried out by the Prison Reform Trust (2012a:2), where it is estimated that women are imprisoned, on average, 55 miles away from their 'home or court of committal court address'.

None of the women in the sample experienced a simple process of dispersal from one place to another. All of the participants were dispersed more than once and, on average, were relocated away from their home communities four times. Some women experienced this repeat dispersal over very long distances. To draw analyses, Natalie's penal pathway shows that she was displaced 116 miles away from her home community to HMP Low Newton on three occasions, and on a fourth occasion she was located 142 miles away to Westhampton Probation hostel, as a condition of her parole license. Belinda's penal pathway shows a similar story. She was located 60 miles away from her home when she was sent to custody in HMP Newhall, and on the second occasion, 150 miles away from home when she was sent to custody at HMP Peterborough. At the time of the interviews being carried out for this study, Belinda was located 34 miles away from her home in Wrexham.

Women's geographical dispersal cannot be measured in miles alone, but by the relative inaccessibility of the places that they are dispersed to. It is important to assess the distance in the time it takes to travel by public transport since, to borrow from Devlin's (1998:78) important analysis of women in prison, 'most women's prisons are so difficult to reach by public transport', even when they appear to be geographically close to their home community. When Belinda was in custody, situated 150 miles from her home community in Wrexham, she had to a travelling time, by public transport, of just under five hours. **Similarly when Shirelle was in custody and** located only 12.3 miles away from her home community, it took Shirelle 1 hour and 7 minutes to return to her home community by public transport. In comparison to Shirelle, it would take another participant, Deborah, to travel only a marginally longer travelling time of 1 hour and 16 minutes to reach her home community which was more than 3 times the distance of Shirelle's dispersal. Both Shirelle and Deborah's penal pathways demonstrate that women's geographical dispersal cannot be measured in miles alone, but by the relative inaccessibility of the places that they are dispersed to.

Contrary to the commonly held view that community punishment enables those who offend to sustain their family and support networks (Bottoms, 1987), this evidence from those interviews shows how women's relationship in 'the community' are interrupted. The practice of dispersal encourages women to sever contact, not only with the perpetrator, but also with their community support networks. This is clearly illustrated by Natalie's penal pathway. As we have seen, she was dispersed 142 miles away from her home community in Cumbria, meaning that Natalie would need to travel over three hours by public transport, from Westhampton to Cumbria, to visit her probation officer. Those experiences, amongst others, indicate that dispersing women to new and unfamiliar surroundings fails to produce any sense of 'belonging' or 'community membership', but conversely estranges women from their support networks and dismembers them from their home community. Given the extent of women's dispersal and the frequency of their upheaval, it is hardly surprising that four out of eight women in this study made plans to be rehoused in Westhampton and resettle there permanently.

Conclusion

Gendered geographies of punishment, as a concept, foregrounds the geographical dispersal of women in the criminal justice system. While the scarcity of probation approved hostels for women present considerable challenges to the practical arrangements of community punishment for women, the gendered phenomenon of dispersing women is more complex. The dispersal of women is given momentum by the blurring of the boundaries between women's need and risk, where these two fields are conceptualised by the criminal justice system as mutually reinforcing characteristics (Barton, 2005), and furthermore, women's risk is tied not only to her history of offending and re-offending but is ultimately tied to their community. Once a woman's community circumstances are triggered as both a risk to causing her harm and leading her to re-offend, the process of dispersal is instantaneously legitimated, moving her, in probationary terms, 'out of area'.

References

Barton. A. and Cooper, V. (2012) 'Hostels and Community Justice for Women: the Semi Penal Paradox' in, M.Malloch and G. McIvor Women, *Punishment and Social Justice: Human Rights and Penal Practices*, London: Routledge

Barton, A. (2005) *Fragile Moralities and Dangerous Sexualities*, Aldershot: Ashgate.

Bottoms, A. E. (1987) 'Limiting Prison Use in England and Wales' *Howard Journal of Criminal Justice,* Vol. 26 No. 3, 177-202

Cooper, V. (*In Review*) 'Gendered Geographies of Punishment' Submitted to *Howard Journal of Criminal Justice*

CJJI (2008) *Probation hostels: Control, Help and Change? A Joint Inspection of Probation Approved Premises,* London: Criminal Justice Joint Inspection

CJJI (2011) *Equal but different? An inspection of the use of alternatives to custody for women offenders,* London: Criminal Justice Joint Inspection

Devlin, A. (1998) *Invisible Women: What's Wrong with Women's Prisons?* Winchester: Waterside Press

Gelsthorpe, L., Sharpe, G. and Roberts, J. (2007) *Provision for Women Offenders in the Community*, London: Fawcett Society

Haney, L. (2010) *Offending Women: Power Punishment and the Regulation of Desire,* California: University of California Press

Hannah-Moffat, K. (2006) 'Pandora's Box: Risk/need and gender-responsive corrections' *Criminology and Public Policy,* Vol. 5, No. 1, 1301-11

HM Inspectorate of Prisons (2005) *Recalled prisoners. A short review of recalled adult male determinate-sentenced prisoners*, London: Her Majesty's Inspectorate of Prisons

Ministry of Justice (2011) *Local Opportunities A Review of Local Solutions for Accommodation Women Offenders in the South West who Pose a High Risk of Harm to Others*, London: Ministry of Justice

Prison Reform Trust (2012) *Women in Prison*, London: Prison Reform Trust

Prison Reform Trust (2014) *Bromley Briefing Factfile*, London: Prison Reform Trust

CHAPTER 3:
Political Detainees In The Philippines: Sustained By Family, The Movement, And Islam

Andrew M. Jefferson

Field-based studies of non-Western prisons are relatively rare which means that our understandings of the experience of prisoners 'beyond the West' are limited. The data presented in this essay are drawn from an ambitious study of the entangled encounters between reform NGOs and prisons in Kosovo, Sierra Leone and the Philippines. The broader study draws on qualitative data (observations, interviews with staff and inmates, reviews of policy documents etc.) gathered by teams of co-researchers working for critical human rights NGOs in the three countries. This essay represents an early attempt to make sense of some of the data gleaned from interviews with political detainees in the Philippines.[1]

As we reviewed the data our attention was drawn to the different ways in which prisoners affiliated to different groups opposed to the state (Leftists and Muslims respectively) struggled to come to terms with their incarceration and orient themselves to the ongoing present moment and the future. The importance of family, the leftist political movement and Islam emerge as central. But what is most striking is the way in which the detainees narrate their current experience in terms of their life trajectories drawing on past experience and looking beyond present moments of suffering towards imagined futures. Immediate misery is not prominent; everyday suffering is contextualized within broader temporal frames featuring senses of both sorrow and injustice.

---

[1] In the Philippines the study is a collaboration between DIGNITY – Danish Institute Against Torture and Balay Rehabilitation Center Inc. I acknowledge my gratitude to co-researchers Merl Moises, Karl Arvin Hapal and Meldz Rebate. The broader study features in the forthcoming book 'Human Rights in Prison: Comparing Institutional Encounters' by Andrew M. Jefferson and Liv S. Gaborit (Palgrave Macmillan)

The data and analysis presented is preliminary and partial in nature and should not be considered exhaustive. It features two of the main carceral establishments in Manila, the New Bilibid Prison (for convicted inmates, run by the Bureau of Corrections) and the Special Intensive Care Area (SICA, for remand prisoners, run by the Bureau of Jail Management and Penology). Since our purpose here is simply to give a flavor of experience rather than situate that experience politically or societally, two quotes, one from each prison, may be sufficient to set the scene. The first gives a sense of the initial reaction to being sentenced (captured through the language of chill and coldness) followed by some small relief when capital punishment was abolished. The second expresses the harshness of the jail experience and its threat to a sense of self:

> *When they read our verdict... the only feeling I felt was the constant chill and the coldness of the sentence. I have lost all hope. We were brought here immediately. At that time, every time they execute someone through lethal injection, everyone becomes restless and anxious... Then came the abolition of capital punishment... When it was finally abolished, my life lightened a little. My dreams of the future for and with my family came back; I had the reason again to look forward to tomorrow....*
> New Bilibid Prison Feb 1 2012

> *In reality, no matter how much flexibility they give us, nor how much they make the jails tolerable for us, it is still a hard life to live inside the jail. We are feeling buryong; the feeling we have never felt before in our lives outside the jail... Buryong is a very problematic feeling. It's like a combination of everything, and your mind becomes troubled and confused and messy.*
> SICA Jan 31st 2012

Both these remarks situate the detainees firmly in time (as well as in space). The latter example looks back, noting that the feeling of *buryong* is something he and his comrades have never felt *before*. The former speaks of dreams of the future and the hope of *looking forward*. It is such statements that drew our initial analytic attention to the ways in which futures were imagined and talked about in interviews.

When asked about their future plans or dreams the leftists almost always linked freedom with family. They do not dream of freedom from the claws of the repressive state as much as they dream of freedom to live up to the obligation they feel to their families. Many of the leftist respondents revealed a deep ambivalence about the political movement combined with a kind of resignation that it was *for* the movement, or *because* of the revolution that they are incarcerated and *to* the movement that they may well return in spite of themselves. There is evidence that despite disillusionment, loss and sorrow the movement still tugs them in the direction of continued political struggle.

We might explain the orientation to family rather than the movement in relation to the splits within the movement outside and inside the prison, the changing political landscape (from the Marcos dictatorship to the so-called emerging democracy of the current regime dominated by elitist family dynasties), and/or in relation to a general despondency brought on by years of incarceration. Alternatively it seems that for some their ambivalence to the movement relates to a perception of neglect or even a sense that they are being used as pawns in factionalised political posturing. As one detainee put it, questioning the sincerity of external agencies and parties:

> *In a way it would be beneficial for them if political prisoners would stay inside because then they would have issues for their campaigns.*
> NBP Feb 1 2012

Muslims held at SICA are in the rather different position of still awaiting conviction or release. What preoccupies them is the circumstances of their arrest and continuing detention. But they find sustenance and inspiration in their faith and shared religious identity. Religious rituals (the prayers, for instance) provide a focal point for resistance and negotiations with the jail authorities. For example, through intensive lobbying the Muslim detainees were able to acquire permission to pray together five times a day which means their cells are opened earlier than those of other detainees but perhaps equally, if not more, importantly, they are able to symbolically express and constitute their sense of collective religious identity. The preparations for prayer are quite striking to an outside observer – the rolling out of brightly-coloured mats on the grey concrete floor below the landings, the donning of robes and the solemn taking up of kneeling positions present a vivid, even incongruous spectacle.

The Muslims are also concerned with family but in a more immediate manner than the Leftists. Coming mainly from the southern islands of the Philippines, the Muslim detainees are either isolated from their families, or their families have uprooted themselves and are residing in deprived neighbourhoods in Manila. As one Muslim detainee at SICA put it when asked about his biggest problem:

> *My heart disease. Not literally though. My heart is sick because I am missing my family so much. That is the worse compared to troubles I am handling being a chairman. Even compared to a fight here, longing for them is the biggest trouble I am facing. I have never cried in my entire life. Not until now. I cry because of my family.*
> March 6 2012

The leftists too spoke powerfully about the pull of family. The following quotes represent typical responses revealing different versions of the tension between family and the movement in an imagined, idealised future:

> *I'll go straight to my family. My principles are still in me, it will never disappear. But I have thought about how we were neglected by our comrades, and it left a mark.* March 13 SICA

> *I want to go back to my family, it's all I wanted. I have lost the interest to continue fighting for my principles. I owed so much from my family... Dwelling on my troubles would do me no good*

anyway so why think about it and lose my interest in life. My family is what I am looking forward to, to keep me going. Feb 15 NBP

The first I'd do is to mend my family and help them improve. I have decided to never go back to being armed. I would still contribute to our struggle but in a different form. And I believe that I have done so much for the movement perhaps they would understand my choice. I have more debt to my family now. Before my mother died, all I ever wanted was to see her. Now that she is gone, I just want to make it up with whose left. Feb 21 NBP

At the same time as speaking about the draw of the family they also spoke of the pull of the movement:

I would definitely go to my family the moment I leave this place. My freedom would be my gift for them. My comrades back in Mindoro are still communicating with me. Sometimes they even ask for some advice on what to do. They still believe in me and my ideas. It is a reason why I still have the feeling of wanting to go back. But unlike before when I dedicated my life to it, I would keep a low profile now. Because in the end, you are not really sure what would happen when you're outside. Feb 1 2012 NBP

You know, I'm not really sure. But I would want to not be harassed the moment I get out of prison, because you can never tell. Even if I say that I want to focus on my children, I could still see the struggle. It is there, it will never stop. I quite know that no matter what, you still have the tendency to go back. Feb 1 2012 NBP

These brief quotes are filled with doubt and hesitancy. The desire, the hope is palpable as is the doubt about its realization.

In the following joint interview with a Muslim and a Leftist detainee the differences in the strategies drawn upon to sustain them during their incarceration come through very clearly:

> Leftist Prisoner: *The government must focus on its prisoners. It must do something to hasten the trials of our cases. Because even if they make the prison feel like staying in a hotel, you are still a prisoner...*

> Researcher: *How do you perceive your detention?*
> Leftist Prisoner: *For us, it is very clear that the state is the enemy and incarceration is part of the people's war. We, fighters, have even accepted the fact that we could die if we are not careful. But the prison is the cemetery of the living. This is a situation that is secondary to death.*

> Muslim Prisoner: *As a Muslim, it is easier for us to accept our situation. This is our destiny; Allah permitted this to happen to us and we have handed over our lives to him because he is the one who knows. Yes, it was very difficult at first, but there is no other choice, besides, nothing will happen if you won't learn to accept your situation. Worse has happened to those detainees who have given in.*

> Leftist Prisoner: *That is the difference with us. We were detained because we are fighting for our principles. With that, it was easier to accept things. If you are optimistic, you would think that for every time you stay here, you are closing in to the day you would be freed.*

However decent the prison is made, says the leftist, you will still be a prisoner. And for him that situation is second only to death. Yet, in contrast to his Muslim interlocutor, his acceptance of the situation is not because he sees it as pre-ordained but because it was always a possible consequence of the principled fight against the regime. Somewhat surprisingly, given what he has said before, the leftist is able to end on an almost positive note. Despite referring to the prison as a cemetery of the living he seems to look on his current experience as though the glass was half-full rather than half-empty. Every day that passes is a day nearer freedom! Reading between the lines of the Muslim interviewee we sense some ambivalence or at least a sense that accepting the situation is not equivalent to giving in. Faith in Allah (who knows) is important for sustaining life and overcoming any tendency to give in. Both men here reach beyond their immediate circumstances, one across time, the other across the oft-neglected spiritual dimension.

Conclusion

The quotes considered above and the cursory analysis offer a brief taste of the richness of the material the co-researchers have been able to collect. What is striking is that the narratives feature more a sense of sorrow, melancholia, loss, sacrifice, and disappointment than misery and despair despite heavy sentences, lengthy periods in *judicial limbo* and personal histories of harsh treatment at the hands of the state. There seems to be more focus in the narratives on the past and the future than on immediate circumstances. This is *not* to say that incarceration is not debilitating or that the immediate present context does not matter. What seems to be the case, however, is that being political detainees - albeit with different orientations - they have an external point of reference (the family, the leftist struggle or Islam) through which to alleviate some of the inevitable and immediate pains of imprisonment.

In closing we want to emphasize that this essay is little more than an appetizer. It makes a small contribution to the increasingly vibrant debates about relations between confinement and subjectivity across the world. It is our hope that subsequent analysis will reveal further subtleties and nuances around these dynamics of prison survival with which other critical scholars of confinement might engage.

CHAPTER 4:
Creating and Managing 'Mad', 'Bad' and 'Dangerous': The Role of Immigration System[1].

Monish Bhatia

> *The welfare of those in our care is always our top
> priority and we take great care to ensure that our
> employees ... were made aware of their
> responsibilities in this respect. Our employees ...
> trained, screened and vetted to the standards
> defined by strict Home Office guidelines. We believe
> that at all times we acted appropriately and in full
> compliance with the terms of our contract with
> UKBA...*
> (G4S Website)

Jimmy Mubenga, a healthy 42 year old man from Angola, died on 12th October 2010 whilst in the custody of three Detention Officers employed by G4S. These private security officers were empowered by statute to use reasonable force to effect a removal. All three officers had training in the use of force and, in particular, in 'Control and Restraint'. That training was contractually required to be delivered and was prescribed by the *"Use of Force"* training manual. According to the evidence produced by INQUEST, a struggle occurred between Mr Mubenga and the three officers and he was in consequence handcuffed in the rear stack position and restrained in a seat. A significant number of witnesses reported that during the final few minutes of his life Mr Mubenga shouted that he could not breathe and "they're killing me" (or similar). He eventually died of a cardio-respiratory collapse due to the 'carpet karaoke' restraint

---

[1] I would like to thank Vickie Cooper, Joe Sim, Steve Tombs, Mary Corcoran, Agniezska Martynowicz, Eloise Cockcroft and Vicky Canning for their questions and comments on the hour long paper presented at the Sites of Confinement conference, from which this short article is extracted.

method. According to a scientific study conducted by Parkes, Thakes and Price (2011), significant reductions in lung function occurred in participants when they were seated restraint in a leant forward position (which also caused Mubenga's death).

The restraint techniques prescribed by G4S were not scientifically proven to be safe. The death of Jimmy Mubenga initiated a long 3-4 year struggle in holding officials accountable, and finally three officers were charged on the grounds of manslaughter in March 2014. However, the Crown Prosecution Service found no basis on which to bring criminal charges for corporate manslaughter against G4S, despite the company's track record (in Britain and across the world) of managing children and adults in its 'care' and pending court cases (also see Fekete, 2011). In 2010 alone, G4S received more than 775 complaints in relation to its detention and deportation of immigrants, including allegations of assaults and racism, with 25 complaints were upheld (after allegations were subjected to "internal investigation"). The UK Prisons Inspector Dame Anne Owers (2001-2010) claimed that conditions in the G4S-run immigration centre are 'objectionable, distressing [and] inhumane' (RedPepper, 2012). Similarly, the evidence from Australia, highlighted in the Human Rights and Equality Commission (HREOC) and other media reports, widely criticises appalling conditions inside detention centres and its effect on detainees physical and mental health. As in the UK, the Australian detention is also managed by a private security company and a subsidiary of the G4S. The company eventually lost its multimillion deportation contract in the UK in 2010 (and retained detention contract, followed by a new contract to manage asylum housing in 2012); nevertheless, the violence during forced removals has continued by other private contractors (Bhatia, PhD).

Cases like that of Mubenga may be an unintended consequence of the practice of deportation, but they still serve the state's ultimate deterrent goal. For each publicised case of a resister suffering death, injury or humiliation encourages many other non-citizens facing deportation to leave passively in order to avoid a similar fate (Gibney, 2013). Despite of the obvious risks, asylum seekers in my research have actively and ferociously resisted detention and deportation, and in process endured violence, days of solitary confinement, becoming labelled as 'dangerous criminals', imprisoned without recourse to fair trial and denial of justice. In this report I will draw upon narratives of victim resistance, case study of one Congolese asylum seeker called John (pseudonym), so as to highlight the extent of suffering and deliberate negligence in detention and during forced removals.

Victim resistance and criminological research

Victim resistance, combined with criminological research, can be crucial in designating particular state activities as criminal, and constructing the social audience that rejects them. For instance, Grewcock questions whether asylum seekers as victims should be the "object" of "neutral" research. Should detainees, for example, be seen primarily as passive victims of state abuse? He strongly indicates that state crime research should acknowledge, if not emphasise, the potential subjective role played by victims, and there is a complex and dynamic inter-relationship between the researcher and the victim that confronts traditional perceptions of criminological research. He further mentions:

> *Immigration detention is undoubtedly a miserable and damaging experience for many but it does not instil total passivity in its victims. Detainees are not merely objects to be pitied or studied, let alone locked up and deported. They have a legitimate sense of entitlement that while not necessarily expressed in the rarefied language of international humanitarian law, is a source of grievance and individual and collective resistance... How, as criminologists and academic researchers committed to highlighting and understanding state crime, do we relate to its victims? ... Are we neutral bystanders attempting to analyse from a distance, eschewing any role as advocates or allies? What role, if any, exists for engaged criminological research?* (Grewcock, 2012:114)

For criminological researchers, engaging with the victims of state crime[2] is not a straightforward process, and the research involving detainees generates its own specific challenges and obstacles, for example, the media coverage tends to follow and reinforce an agenda established explicitly by government officials operating within a stifling mainstream political consensus (ibid; also see Pickering, 2005:15). With regards to this, Fekete (2012) has mentioned that

> *over the years it has become much more difficult to get asylum protests reported: news has to be different to be newsworthy. As the grim facts facing asylum seekers are pretty constant, editors, even those who sympathise with asylum seekers and migrants, will most often respond to a journalist seeking to cover a hunger strike, or an occupation, by asking 'what's different?' The response is the same when journalists seek to cover detention protests, where detainees barricade themselves into their cells and set fire to their mattresses, or even self-harm. As a further indication of these attitudes, the Institute of Race Relations spoke to an NGO representative who told us that once when she approached an editor to ask if he would cover a 'riot' in a detention centre she was told 'it's only news if someone dies'. The immigration authorities, for their part, are quick to dismiss hunger strikes and suicide attempts as incidents of deviance, attention-seeking and predictable acts of manipulation.*

Such official pronouncements can be accepted uncritically by the media as authoritative statements. An editor at one of the UK's leading liberal newspapers mentioned of an unsolicited piece that editorial policy was not to cover hunger strikes by asylum-seekers, on the grounds that the tactic was unfair and protesters were not playing by the rules (see Carr,

---

[2] Pickering (2005) and Grewcock (2010) have used Green and Ward's (2004) definition of 'state organised deviance involving violation of human rights', to critique and challenge treatment of asylum seekers by liberal democratic states.

2012). While visits to detainees by members of the public are still possible, it is often subjected to endless bureaucracies and made difficult through actual distance from the detention sites. This does not mean that the voices of the detainee are entirely absent from the public record; it is nevertheless fragmented and extensively mediated through court records, the reports of human rights organisations and the publicity efforts of campaign groups and support networks (Grewcock 2009: 217–41). The absence of consistent opportunities for detainees and deportees to engage in open public discussion underlines the practical obstacles to victim research and reinforces the need for researchers to consciously *claim a space for victim agency* and challenge the state deviance from below.

Research Findings

Overall, this research[3] examined the impacts of UK immigration policies and procedures on asylum seekers and 'illegal' migrants. In-depth interviews with twenty two asylum seekers and six specialist practitioners were undertaken to gain in-depth experiential information. As an established volunteer support worker with three refugee organisations over a period of eighteen months, I was able to research participants and interact with state authorities, and gathered a rich qualitative data set. The following section outlines powerful narrative of resistance of one asylum seeker called John and the extent of abuse that he endured in detention centres and while being forcefully removed from the country.

John's story of resistance and 'crime'

> *"My life was in danger in Congo … in [UK] detention I was a danger and treated like a black murderer!"*
> (Interview with John)

John was fleeing torture and persecution. He applied for asylum in 2002 and was dispersed to the North East of

---

[3] PhD study was undertaken between 2009 and 2013 at the University of Huddersfield

England. He was asked by accommodation provider (sub-contractor) to share a bed with another male asylum seeker - which he refused. The landlord then asked him to leave the premises. Having been subjected to torture, John was experiencing severe physical and mental health issues, and threatened to commit suicide. The landlord sought assistance from the police and John was charged and taken into custody. The next morning he appeared in the Court on a public order offence; however, the Judge took a decision in favour of John and requested for his re-dispersal to another suitable location. He started living in Midlands, but his address was not changed on the Home Office database. John's case was eventually rejected and he was evicted from the property and started living on streets and sleeping in local buses. Throughout this time he was under the impression that decision on his case was yet to be made. During the fieldwork it was noted that on several occasions the Home Office failed to record correct addresses. Also, asylum seekers who were made destitute found it difficult to keep track of case related correspondence due to lack of access to the property. Both of these result in missing court hearings and other important notifications. In the case of John, the inability to respond and take prompt action on the Home Office letters not only resulted in case refusal but also being labelled as 'absconder' and an 'illegal' migrant.

John was destitute for over a year and was caught travelling on a local bus without a valid ticket. He was taken to the nearest police station for finger prints, and charged with 'absconding' and living 'illegally'. After spending 72 hours in the police cell, he was transferred to the detention centre, and a few days later he started protesting for his release. At this point he was physically assaulted by the detention officers and kept isolated in a secured cell. He later initiated a naked hunger strike, and also covered the walls with his own faeces, and vandalised the physical space of the detention camp. He explained:

> ...they pushed me into the cell. I just got all my clothes off and make hunger strike. I was so angry that I shit and spread the shit all over the walls. I was there for 5 days. They told me if you don't

behave we will keep you here forever. I said no
problem. I continued my hunger strike and I did not
even drink water.
(Interview with John)

This act of vandalism (or resistance) was met with a swift removal order. On the seventh day of hunger strike, eight private security company officers escorted John to the airport so as to forcefully remove him from the country. This move was resisted by John, resulting in further physical violence by the authorities. As described during the interview:

On my 7ᵗʰ day of hunger strike they sent eight BIG
security people to deport me... They beat me again,
very hard. They took me to the Heathrow airport for
deportation in the Ethiopian Airline flight. They said
you have to go, and I said 'NO' I can't go. They kept
screaming yes, and I said 'no I can't go'. They took
me to cabin; they put fingers inside my nose and
pulled it. I was bleeding very badly AHH AHHH
[sound of pain]. Eight of them forced me inside the
flight and kept slapping me in front of the pilot and
air hostess. They told the pilot and air hostess that I
am ready for getting deported. Pilot said 'no, I
cannot take a screaming and bleeding passenger on
this flight'. They asked me to get 'calm' and said
that 'I will have to go'- I said 'no I can't go'. I was
bleeding from my nose, they hit me very hard. They
punch me PWOAR [sound of a loud bang]. They tie
my hands, they tie my legs...
(Interview with John)

According to Grewcock (2009) force involved during removals often includes techniques that would constitute a serious assault in other circumstances. There is little readily available data to indicate how routinely such methods of restraint are used by the officials in Britain and across the West in general. However, it is clear that such expulsions are one way process and it removes asylum seekers from the Western state and which absolves itself of any further responsibility – as there is no monitoring mechanism set in place which foresees the circumstances under which these individuals are forcefully removed (ibid). Similarly, the report 'Outsourcing of Abuse' outlines the lack of transparency around the contracts between the Home Office and private companies, which the Home Office states is justified for commercial reasons.

Due to the failed removal attempt, John was taken back to the detention centre, where he once again started resisting his confinement and initiated a hunger strike along with other male detainees, which somehow managed to grab the media attention. He was questioned by the police officers regarding his involvement in the strike, and was then transferred to prison for violating the detention rules (and becoming a potential 'danger' for other detainees due to his active protests and disruptive behaviour). He spent over 3 months in the Category B prison, without being subjected to trial proceedings. One of the official documents stated the following reasons in support of the decision to keep him in prison facilities:

> In light of his behaviour and threats ... he was no longer suitable to be detained in an Immigration Removal Centre...allegations of abuse [against him] are currently under investigation.
>
> (Home Office, date anonymised)

It is noted that subsequent immigration legislation has 'created' several offences, which have expanded and transferred police-like powers to the immigration (and related) officers. As a result of which, assaulting a private security/detention officer, and obstructing immigration officer(s) is a punishable offence, and replicates the ones related to constables and prison officers. Such powers provide immigration officers with leverage to enforce compliance, and were requested by operational officers who found it 'helpful' to have their authority backed up with a criminal sanction (Aliverti, 2012). Similarly, Grewcock (2010) highlights that acts of resistance often result in disciplinary sanctions, including prolonged confinement in segregation units within the detention centres and transfers to prisons; others have resulted in criminal prosecutions and harsh prison sentences. Such responses reinforce the deviance vested in detainees by virtue of their detention and used to legitimise the bitterly punitive response to asylum seekers and 'illegal' migrants. The official response to these events is focused on the potential criminality of the detainees "contumacious behaviour" (Grewcock, 2012:110).

Due to repeated protests in the detention centre, John was 'othered' and labelled as a 'troublemaker', 'danger' and a 'security threat'. According to analysis of the data, every act of resistance and protest intensified this 'othering'- and triggered a cycle of further 'criminality' within the detention camp. John was eventually considered as a 'serious offender'; however, he had not committed any 'serious crime'. Several letters[4] from the Members of Parliament raised this issue with Her Majesty's Prison Services and received no immediate and/or clear response (besides that he was a 'threat'- with no clear justification behind the use of this term). Nevertheless, John's mental health continued to deteriorate and he increasingly turned suicidal in a Category B prison, and was forced into a segregation unit - as he explained:

> *I was treated like a prisoner. They put me in the segregation unit, with no television, you cannot mix with people and I was left alone. I kept screaming that 'I am not a prisoner, why have you put me in this cell'. Then one day the prison governor came and said that he 'cannot do anything, and that it is an immigration situation'... I was taken out of prison [eventually] and into the detention centre [again].*
> (Interview with John)

According to the documentary analysis, John was receiving assistance from two organisations and at the same time writing to local MPs about his situation and psychological state, with a hope that release will be granted. When he eventually applied for immigration bail, the Home Office Presenting Officer referred to his files and written notes drafted by the G4S officials, and requested that the judge

---

[4] John had consented to obtaining copies of his case-files from the criminal solicitor. The documents consisted of John's immigration and 'criminal' history.

refuse the bail application, as his behaviour showed a *"blatant disregard for authority and does not possess a compliant nature as such... not a suitable candidate for release"* (Bail Summary). John continued to be detained and he kept protesting for his release. He contacted a number of journalists to raise awareness of the treatment in detention centres. This created further problems, as mentioned in one of the letters written to the MPs:

> *...was talking to the newspaper reporters on the phone regarding a detainee who had killed himself...the officers called me fucking black and physically attacked me. I was punched and beaten by officers who twisted my arms and legs...the two officers called for reinforcements and suddenly 12 officers appeared...after I was stripped naked and handcuffed, the twelve officers also assisted in my beating...I have scars to prove what I am saying...as I was stripped naked in full view of all officers including women...looking at me as if I was not a human being..."*
> (Interview with John)

During this incident, John was accused of physically assaulting a detention officer (which was also recorded in his detention file) and transferred to a 'maximum security prison' (or Category A) without being charged or subjected to a trial. When the MPs requested an explanation for not charging and/or offering him a fair trial, the Home Office responded: *"... have chosen not to prosecute so as to allow the Border Agency to pursue his removal expediently"* (Home Office, date anonymised). After spending over a week there, the prison governor concluded that John was 'vulnerable' and 'at-risk' in the maximum security prison, and asked the Home Office to arrange for his release. John was then transferred to a Category B prison (again) where he spent over a year. His bail applications were refused as he was now a 'serious threat' (who was previously held in the 'maximum security prison'), and the deportation order reinstated. However, on this occasion the Home Office arranged for a chartered flight from a different airport - as he mentioned:

During early morning hours, around four in the morning, there were nine police officers and they came with six vans to escort me to the [anon] airport for deportation. I was shackled like American prisoner, there was chain around my legs, and I was handcuff. People at the airport were surprised... they thought that I was a terrorist. ...They said 'it is too hard to deport you [on a commercial flight] from Heathrow, so we have to send you to a European destination [in a charter flight] and from there you will go to Congo'. It was like being a notorious criminal. [John later started protesting at the European airport and was bought back to the UK.]

They [Home Office officials] said 'ok, we will transfer you to the prison because you are trouble maker and you are not willing to co-operate'. I said 'no problem'. I was taken to London prison for six months.
(Interview with John)

Throughout his time in prison, John wrote to over 50 letters to MPs, the Prime Minister, and members of the royal family, pleading for his release. However, in all of these instances, the recipients of the letters established contact with the Home Office[5], who referred to his case files (which were partially drafted by the private security companies) and justified his confinement as a 'security issue'. John was eventually released and he spent over one month in the psychiatric unit receiving treatment for nervous breakdown. After the discharge he was dispersed to the North of England for a short time (and was interviewed by the researcher). Nevertheless, during a reporting event in 2011, he was once again taken back to the detention centre and spent over a year in confinement and was subject to further abuses for protesting, resisting and being disruptive.

---

[5] It was mentioned in every letter that Home Office was contacted for further information and clarification of John's case. The researcher was provided with documentary evidence and copies of these letters.

The end is the beginning

John was eventually released (again) on mental health grounds and he is currently awaiting decision on his asylum case. He is very active, does voluntary work with several charity organisations, and gives public talks on state violence and the harms of detention. Through his talks he has tried to raise awareness of the hidden and dark side of detention centres and its impact on asylum seeking individuals. As a survivor, being able to speak in public about his experiences (and also with the researcher during interview) demonstrated the on-going struggle to reclaim and reconstruct his life, and construct state activities as deviant. John continues to resist and challenge the status quo[6].

Throughout my research, asylum seekers and 'illegal' migrants have constantly resisted practices and also inflicted violence upon their bodies to make their voices heard. For instance, an Iranian asylum seeker called Ali (pseudonym)went on a 2 week hunger strike after being released from the prison, and continued his acts of resistance, and demanded for a decision on his 5 year old asylum case- as mentioned:

> *One of the main reasons behind my hunger strike was to show how hard is life for me...that I can put my life in danger... ready to die...I can't take this life... I went on hunger strike!...Home Office then refused my case with a 'right to appeal'...I wanted a decision on my case and they gave me that decision...now if I died hungry, it would not be their responsibility anymore...I ended up breaking my hunger strike and continued [fight] for my freedom...*
> (Interview with Ali)

The authorities once again refused his application while he was on hunger strike, initiating the cycle of judicial appeals. After much struggle, he finally received his refugee status in late 2011. Ali is now doing a degree in sciences at one of the

---

[6] In a similar way, In an agreed to join the researcher to give a talk at the Manchester Metropolitan University. He highlighted the trauma and suffering in the UK, failed suicide attempts and ways in which system tried to reduce him to 'bare-life' and ways in which he survived the atrocities inflicted by the British state.

top 20 universities in the UK. Similarly, Rizwan, Mustafa, Inam, Anthony, Rafiq, Ahmed. Mahmood and Iqbal, all received their refugee status during the course of this research, having had to wait for between five and ten years and after enduring significant time in prison and detention centres. Their cases will be discussed in future articles. By using case studies, this article has highlighted some of the systematic abuses and harms inflicted by the British state and the damaging consequences of coercive controls on asylum seekers. It was noted that violence is endemic, widespread and perhaps hidden within the system, and further research is needed to expose and challenge the status-quo and contribute to the on-going resistance to state crimes.

References

Agamben, G. (1998) *Homo Sacer: Sovereign Power and Bare Life*, Stanford University Press

Aliverti, A. (2012) *Making People Criminal: The Role of the Criminal Law in Immigration Enforcement*, in *Theoretical Criminology*, Vol. 16, No. 4, 417-434

Fekete, L. (2003) *Accelerated removals: the Human Cost of EU Deportation Policies*, in *Race & Class*, Vol. 52 No.4:89-97

Fekete, L. (2012) *From Despair Comes Resistance*, from: http://www.irr.org.uk/news/from-despair-comes-resistance/ (last accessed on 09/01/2013)

Gibney, M. J. (2013) *Is Deportation a Form of Forced Migration?* in *Refugee Quarterly Survey*, Vol. 32, No. 2:116-129

Green, P., & Ward, T. (2005) *State Crime: Government, Violence and Corruption*, Pluto Press, London

Grewcock, M. (2012) *Public Criminology, Victim Agency and Researching State Crime*, State Crime. Vol. 1. No. 1:109-125

Grewcock, M. (2010) *Border Crimes: Australia's War on Illicit Migrants* in The Federation Press, Institute of Criminology: Sydney

Hunt, T. (2012) *G4S: Private Muscle for Hire* from http://www.redpepper.org.uk/g4s-private-muscle-for-hire/ (last accessed on 09/01/2013)

Parkes. J., Thakes, D., and Price, M. (2011) Effect of Seated Restraint and Body Size on Lung Function, from: http://iapdeathsincustody.independent.gov.uk/wp-content/uploads/2011/08/Effect-of-seated-restraint-and-body-size-on-lung-function-Parkes-Thake-Price-2011.pdf (last accessed on 10/11/2013)

Pickering, S. (2005) *Refugees & State Crime*, The Federation Press, Sydney Institute of Criminology

CHAPTER 5:
Detention and asylum: who safeguards our most vulnerable people?

Eloise Cockcroft

Introduction

This chapter outlines challenges faced by people seeking asylum in the United Kingdom. It focuses specifically on the treatment of applicants living with mental health problems, and explores the problems they can face in accessing health-care, both within the community and within detention centres, as well as factors which can affect the prospects of long-term recovery in the UK.

Through the lens of a case study, barriers to accessing health care will be addressed, specifically in relation to finding a voice with which to express individual psycho-social needs. The efforts of social workers from voluntary organisations to advocate on their behalf will also be identified. This particular insight is facilitated through my own role as social worker with *Revive*[1], a non-governmental organisation which provides practical and social support and legal advice for asylum seekers, refugees, and other vulnerable migrants in order to promote and protect their human rights.

Psycho-social support for people seeking asylum

The term "asylum" literally means "place of refuge". Its legal definition is the protection granted by a state to someone who has left their home country as a refugee for reasons consistent with the Geneva Convention.[2] The

---

[1] Revive is involved with the training of medical professionals around best practice in the care of asylum seekers and refugees. Revive also takes part in the training of UKBA staff to improve decision-making around asylum applications. We campaign with service users for an end to destitution of asylum seekers in the UK.

majority of people who access Revive's social work service experience psychological and mental health problems caused by trauma experienced in his/her country of origin, which is often further compounded by difficulties experienced in the UK. Revive's services include one-to-one long-term support with social workers, helping with identified needs such as signposting to other specialist voluntary sector organisations, accessing statutory health and social care services and advocacy, especially with the UK Border Agency. Social workers and volunteers accompany service users to important appointments and appeal hearings and undertake home visits when necessary. Social workers also run drop-in centres. A warm welcome and opportunities to socialise are provided at the centres by a dedicated team of volunteers as well as lunch, emergency food parcels, clothing and advice from qualified workers. We receive referrals to our social work department from services such as Clinical Psychologists, statutory Mental Health services and Freedom from Torture.

Research by Grey et al (2010) indicates that asylum seekers and refugees who have been treated inhumanely in their country of origin have a higher chance of recovery when they are accepted in to community networks in the host country as well as provided with access to appropriate services and legal recognition as refugees because this provides a sense of safety and a chance to rebuild lives. As they argue, "Factors in exile such as social isolation and unemployment are stronger predictors of depressive morbidity than trauma factors. Identified risk factors for development of PTSD and depression include a loss of social network, fear of repatriation and family separation" (Grey et al., 2010:180). Survivors of torture are more likely to suffer from psychological problems associated with trauma than other refugees (Craig, 2010:14). Long-term psychological therapies and in some cases psychiatric medication have been proven to be effective for the treatment of asylum

---

[2] A refugee is a person who 'Owing to a well-founded fear of being persecuted for reasons of race, religion, nationality, membership of a particular social group, or political opinion, is outside the country of his nationality, and is unable to or, owing to such fear, is unwilling to avail himself of the protection of that country' (Article 1, 1951 Convention Relating to the Status of Refugees). In the UK an asylum seeker is someone who has asked the Government for refugee status and is waiting to hear the outcome of their application (www.unhcr.org.uk).

seekers and refugees with PTSD and other mental health problems (Kinzie, 2010:131-133).

Sites of Confinement: Detention of Asylum Seekers with Mental Health Problems

This brings us to consider detention of asylum seekers in the UK. According to official United Kingdom Border Agency (UKBA) policy asylum applicants who have suffered torture should not be confined in a detention centre unless there are "exceptional circumstances"[3] due to the stresses placed upon the detained person.   This includes individuals with independent evidence of torture and those with a medical condition which cannot be satisfactorily treated in detention. However, a High Court Ruling last year (17th May 2013) called UKBA to account for not following its own policies. In each of these five test cases, the detainees said they had been unlawfully detained because of a systematic failure by UKBA staff to take the medical assessment process seriously. Medical evidence of torture had been ignored. The cases centered on the use of "Rule 35"[4] reports. If a doctor has concerns about the mental or physical well-being of a detainee in a detention centre according to law a "Rule 35" report has to be filed.[5] The judge in these High Court cases said that the system was "not working as it should" and Rule 35 reports had not been filed. The ruling declared that each of the men seeking asylum had been unlawfully detained by UKBA and they were subsequently released. All the claimants in the High Court case had been able to establish the unlawfulness of their detention through the assistance of Medical Justice, who provided access to independent medical experts.[6]

---

[3] Section 55.10 of the UKBA's Enforcement Instructions and Guidance lists groups of people who are considered suitable for detention only in very exceptional circumstances.
[4] Rule 35 lays out requirements for practitioners working with detained asylum seekers. Further information available here:
https://www.gov.uk/government/uploads/system/uploads/attachment_data/file/257437/rule35reports.pdf
[5] The Detention Centre Rules 2001
[6] In 2012, Medical Justice published a detailed report "The Second Torture" which found that the safeguards to identify victims of torture were failing at every stage and that torture survivors were routinely being detained in breach of Home Office policy.

National Health Service (NHS) staff, both within the community and within detention centres, require adequate training and support in how to assess, diagnose and care for asylum seekers and refugees who are presenting with Post Traumatic Stress Disorder (PTSD) and other mental health problems. **I have found during my social work with asylum seekers and refugees at Revive that** patients are sometimes initially diagnosed with stress-related conditions such as "adjustment disorder"[7] when they may be in fact presenting with symptoms which could be indicative of Post-Traumatic Stress Disorder which is a more severe psychological condition that in some cases can cause the onset of acute mental illness (Kinzie, 2010:124). It is crucial that individuals receive appropriate support and/or treatment and follow up care following such a diagnosis.

The treatment of asylum seekers and refugees experiencing complex trauma is the subject of considerable debate within Western psychiatry. There may be significant cultural factors which can complicate the assessment process and the appropriate diagnosis and on-going care of refugee populations, as well as debates around the Western-centricity of PTSD and psychiatry more generally (Grey et al, 2010:178-180). However, it is almost universally acknowledged by psychiatrists that refugee survivors of torture can experience ongoing psycho-social impacts of such abuses, which may be compounded by difficulties in accessing mental health services and long-term, multi-disciplinary therapies as needed (Cross et al, 2010:100-101).

---

[7] 'Adjustment Disorder is an abnormal and excessive reaction to an identifiable life stressor. The reaction is more severe than would normally be expected, and can result in significant impairment in social, occupational or academic functioning' (www.psychologytoday.com/conditions/adjustment-disorder).

The Impact of Detention through the Lens of a Case Study

In 2012, Mohammed[8], a user of Revive's drop-in service, was forcibly "removed"[9] from the UK around two weeks after he was admitted to hospital suffering from what may have been an acute psychotic episode. He had been refused asylum from a Middle Eastern country and his case was that he had been ill-treated and he feared retuning there. When he had been interviewed by UKBA during his asylum claim he had found it difficult to give a clear account of what had happened to him, due to his psychological difficulties and lack of trust in UKBA officials following a history of persecution. He had been street homeless for months when he came to our drop-in service with a friend and he said that he survived mostly by eating out of bins. His UKBA accommodation had been terminated following the refusal of his asylum case and he informed staff that he carried his legal papers in a plastic bag which he kept in a bush where he slept at night-time. When he came to the drop-in centre every week he was offered food, advice and access to interpreters as he spoke little English.

Mohammed seemed very distressed when he came to the centre, but over the course of a few sessions he built up a trusting relationship with workers. He showed social workers scars from where he had self-harmed previously by burning himself on his arms. He was withdrawn and workers observed that he appeared to be hearing voices or responding to auditory hallucinations. He was very scared to seek medical help but after a drop-in session where he appeared particularly disturbed a social worker encouraged him to go to the Accident and Emergency Department of the local hospital because he was clearly in urgent need of medical attention. The drop-in centre was closed early that day when the social worker who had been allocated as his key worker accompanied Mohammed to hospital.

---

[8] I refer to the service user in the following case-study as "Mohammed". This is a pseudonym to protect his identity.
[9] Removal is a process whereby immigration officers enforce return from the UK to another country.

During the mental health assessment at the hospital it was apparent that Mohammed's self-care was very poor and he told staff that he thought that others were telling him to harm himself. According to medical notes his initial diagnosis following this assessment was of "agitated depression" and he was admitted for one week to a psychiatric ward as a voluntary patient. He was observed on the ward to be passive and not to eat much. He expressed suicidal thoughts and occasional hallucinations. No medication was prescribed and he was assessed as suffering from a possible "adjustment disorder". He didn't have access to an interpreter throughout medical assessments at the hospital, despite his obvious difficulties in expressing himself in English.

During the time that Mohammed stayed on the hospital ward, his social worker rang the hospital twice to try to discuss options for his accommodation on discharge such as applying to the local authority's No Recourse to Public Funds department for temporary housing, but she found it difficult to communicate with the hospital. Only a week later he was discharged and he was picked up directly from the hospital ward by UK Border Agency staff who had been informed by hospital staff of his presence there. An out-patients appointment with a psychiatrist had been arranged by the hospital for one week later but Mohammed could not attend this because UK Border Agency took him to a detention centre two hundred miles away.

All medical services at that time within the detention centre were provided by a private company. Mohammed was initially seen there by a General Practitioner (GP) and according to medical notes he was extremely withdrawn and scared. He told the GP that he was suffering from hallucinations which he didn't feel he could discuss much, of people hitting him, telling him to stay away from people and voices telling him not to speak. The GP decided that he was suffering from a psychotic disorder and prescribed him anti-psychotic medication. However, *a Rule 35 report was not submitted* and his detention continued.

Mohammed was seen the following day by a detention centre psychiatrist for a further assessment and he was diagnosed as having a possible 'personality disorder' with 'no sign of psychosis'.   The anti-psychotic medication was discontinued and he received no further medical care from detention centre staff. At the request of his social worker Medical Justice arranged for an independent doctor to see Mohammed at the detention centre. According to this medical report he appeared to be suffering from 'thought disorder' and he could not explain his history and his background well. The report stated that Mohammed was still responding to hallucinations and that he expressed strong suicidal thoughts and appeared to be very traumatised. The doctor concluded that he may have been suffering from schizophrenia and stated within the report that Mohammed was acutely mentally unwell and that he was unable to care for himself but that with appropriate medication and follow up care he could recover in the long-term. The report also warned that without treatment or support 'Mohammed was at severe risk of coming to harm' **and that he was not well enough to travel any substantial distance**.

Under Rule 35 guide-lines, as part of UKBA's duty of care for detainees who may be mentally unwell and unable to provide a coherent account of their difficulties, medical staff should consult with family and friends or other professionals who may be able to provide a history and background information. Mohammed's social worker urgently faxed over a letter to the detention centre expressing concerns for his well-being. The letter stated that he had told staff that he had been ill-treated in his country of origin and it questioned the legitimacy of his continuing detention, considering how acutely mentally unwell he appeared to be. A response to this letter from UKBA has to date not been received.

The Medical Justice report written by the independent doctor was urgently faxed to UKBA by legal representatives following their assessment. It could have formed the basis for a fresh asylum claim but due to the speed of the "removal" process it did not reach UKBA in time to stop the flight. Mohammed was expelled from the UK at the end of 2012, days after he had been admitted to the detention centre and around two years after he had come to the UK. He was forcibly taken back to the country from which he had fled. We have not heard from him again and his last contact with my organisation took place when he rang his social worker and informed her that he had been detained. His future is at best uncertain because he did not have any contact with family or friends who could have cared for him and mental health services in his country of origin are very limited.

A complaint was submitted by Revive last year to the hospital which cared for Mohammed prior to his transfer to the detention centre. A response was received following a detailed investigation which recognised that there were shortcomings in Mohammed's care. The hospital said that the purpose of contacting UK Border Agency was to "make arrangements for Mohammed's accommodation" and staff were not aware that UK Border Agency would detain him. The hospital staff stated that they thought they were acting according to his "best interests". However, the term "best interests" is usually used by professionals where there are questions about a patient's mental capacity to make their own decisions. Under the provisions of the Mental Capacity Act, in these particular cases any family and all professionals involved in the care of the patient should be consulted regarding the best option for discharge.[10] Although Mohammed was unwell, he was well aware of where he was and where he didn't wish to be. He requested help from his social worker to get out of the detention centre as soon as he arrived, so he was certainly capable of making his own decisions and he was fearful of detention due to his experiences in his country of origin which was why he had been reluctant to be admitted to hospital.

The hospital investigation found that there had been a breach of confidentiality because Mohammed had not consented to ward staff contacting UK Border Agency on his behalf and he was not consulted about this. The investigating officer included in her recommendations that hospital staff should receive further training on the care of people seeking asylum and that the member of staff who disclosed Mohammed's location to UK Border Agency should have supervision with his line manager "to review his decision making in relation to the Code of Practice in respect of Patient Confidentiality." The investigating officer also found that the lack of access to interpreters was a concern and that

---

[10] Mental Capacity Act 2005 (www.legislation.gov.uk)

communication by hospital staff with Mohammed's social worker was inadequate.

As from April 2013 responsibility for health-care in detention centres has been transferred from private companies to the NHS commissioner. This is a welcome change because standards of health-care *should* be raised and detention centres will be regularly inspected just as prisons are. Healthcare complaints procedures should fall into line with the rest of the NHS, although it is of course very difficult for a person to make a complaint when UKBA has **expelled them from the UK**. The ultimate decision to release or to forcibly return a sick person who is in detention will still lie with the UKBA which has targets to meet (Burnett, 2000: 26). UKBA continues to allow discredited private companies such as G4S and SERCO to run detention centres.

It seems that the combination of factors leading to Mohammad's detention and expulsion from the UK built up to a perfect storm. An adult with a history of ill-treatment and psychological problems became acutely mentally unwell following the refusal of his asylum case and subsequent destitution. He was let down by mental health services both within the hospital and at the detention centre prior to his forced departure from the UK. He was given several different diagnoses by medical professionals within a short space of time and he was discharged from mental health services when he would have benefited from a long-term period of assessment, follow-up care from mental health services and psychological therapies. He made contact with mental health services at a time of crisis which was crucial for his long-term recovery and this could have led to his rehabilitation within the community and possibly a fresh claim for asylum.

Conclusion: individual, but perhaps not unique

Mohammed, like many asylum seekers living with mental health problems whilst adapting to a new system and host country, struggled to articulate and assert his needs. He tried to find a community which could address the issues he faced and support him in his recovery. He was temporarily provided with crisis support from his social worker but he would have benefited from long-term social work support as planned. Mohammed fled his country with the expectation that he would be protected from further harm. This government rejected his application for refugee status and failed to recognise his right to be treated in a dignified way in the UK with due legal process.

Worryingly, Mohammed's case, although individual, is not unique but indicative of wider experiences of the asylum system. It is a cause for concern that there have been recent incidences such as the case highlighted within this article where medical staff, when faced with the dilemma of how and where to discharge a homeless patient with a refused asylum application, liaised with immigration departments with outcomes that were detrimental to the well-being and safety of the individuals concerned. A fuller assessment of medical and social care needs within the hospital could have led to an eventual grant of asylum for Mohammed. Although Mohammed was admitted to hospital as a voluntary patient, he was soon after deprived of his liberty. His cursory treatment by the hospital led to his subsequent detention and summary removal from the UK.

It is already common practice for local authority social workers when approached by destitute asylum seekers and their families for accommodation and financial support to contact UKBA to check immigration status in order to assess eligibility for services, which can sometimes trigger removal proceedings. The immigration system is undoubtedly placing increasing pressures upon staff caring for asylum seekers within statutory mental health and social care settings. There is an important role for staff within voluntary organisations to work in partnership with medical and social care professionals on behalf of asylum seekers with mental health problems to try to ensure that the "best interests" of these vulnerable individuals can be protected.

It is unfortunate that it is only *after* Mohammed's departure from the UK that this secondary account of his experiences as a refused asylum seeker with mental health problems, by a worker from an organisation which tried to support him, can be evaluated by researchers and campaigners. We may feel that as workers we can ultimately be frustrated in our attempts to support asylum seekers in the face of such an oppressive immigration system. However, it is still important to recognise that positive outcomes can arise from opportunities such as this to bear witness to their stories.

There is currently an enquiry in to the legitimacy of immigration detention by The All-Party Parliamentary Group on Refugees and the All-Party Parliamentary Group on Migration which will include an investigation in to the health-care of detainees. A report has been submitted to the APPG which includes evidence from the case-study outlined in this article. Oppressive immigration legislation enforcing destitution, detention and in some cases expulsion from the UK of traumatised asylum seekers in need of urgent mental health care should and must be challenged.

References

Boyles, J. (2006) *Not Just Naming the Injustice- Counselling Asylum Seekers and Refugees*, in G. Protor *et al* (ed) Politicising the Person-Centred Approach: An Agenda for Social Change. Ross-on-Wye: PCCS Books.

Burnett, J. (2010) *Repatriation Medicine*, in Criminal Justice Matters. Vol.82, Issue 1.

Craig, T (2002) *Mental Distress and Psychological Interventions in Refugee Populations*, in D. Bhugra, T. Craig and K. Bhui. (ed) Mental Health of Refugees and Asylum Seekers Oxford University Press.

Cross, S. Crabb, J. and Jenkins, R. (2002) *International Refugee Policy* in in D. Bhugra, T. Craig and K. Bhui. (ed) Mental Health of Refugees and Asylum Seekers Oxford University Press.

Fell, B. and P. (2013) *Welfare Across Borders: A Social Work Process with Adult Asylum Seekers* in British Journal of Social Work 1-18.

Grey, N. Lab, D. and Young, K. (2010) *Post Traumatic Stress Disorder* in D. Bhugra, T. Craig and K. Bhui. (ed) Mental Health of Refugees and Asylum Seekers Oxford University Press.

Kinzie, J.D. and J.M, (2010) *Treatment goals and therapeutic interactions* in D. Bhugra, T. Craig and K. Bhui. (ed) <u>Mental Health of Refugees and Asylum Seekers</u> Oxford University Press.

Medical Justice Report: (2012) *"The Second Torture": The Immigration Detention of Torture Survivors* London: Medical Justice

Nayak, S, Revive and the Salford Forum for Refugees and People Seeking Asylum United for Change Campaign Group, (2012) *Testimony, Tolerance and Hospitality: The Limitations of the HRA in Relation to Asylum Seekers*, in N. Kang-Riou, J. Milner, and S. Nayak (eds) <u>Confronting the Human Rights Act 1998: Contemporary Themes and Perspectives</u>. Abingdon, Routledge.

Patel, N. and Mahtani, A. (2007) *The politics of working with refugee survivors of torture* in <u>The Psychologist</u>, Vol 20, No.3.

CHAPTER 6:
Exploring the 'Edges of What is Possible'[1]: Abolitionist Activism and Neoliberal Austerity

Joe Sim

> *Abolitionism is a movement to end systemic violence, including the interpersonal vulnerabilities and displacements that keep the system going. In other words, the goal is to change how we interact with each other and the planet by putting people before profits, welfare before warfare, and life over death* (Berger, 2014: vii-viii)

In the second decade of the twenty-first century, as the 'iron times' (Hall, 1988: vii) ushered in by Thatcherism have become further institutionalised and intensified under successive New Labour and Coalition governments, it has become commonplace for the powerful to dismiss the views and actions of abolitionists. This process of disqualification, operating through what Henry Giroux has called a 'disimagination machine' (Truth Out, n.d.), has been profound in that arguments for radical alternatives to the current baleful situation are dismissed as the fantasies of utopian idealists, out of touch with the prevailing, free market orthodoxies and the concerns of 'ordinary' people, one of which is the demand for more law and better order. Allied to this process, are the 'unprecedented levels of secrecy, obfuscation and downright lying' that have become central to the capitalist state's relationship with contemporary politics and culture (Pantich and Leys, 2005: viii).

However, in England and Wales over the last four decades, abolitionists have challenged the socially constructed, idealistic stereotypes generated by the state. In practice,

---

[1] This phrase was used by Attallah Salah-El cited in Meiners (2011: 5). A longer version of this paper can be accessed in Jewkes, Y. (2014) (ed) Handbook on Prisons London: Routledge (with Ryan, M.)

abolitionist interventions have significantly influenced a number of policy debates surrounding prisons. In 1970, the formation of the first abolitionist group, *Radical Alternatives to Prison (RAP)*, was followed by the emergence of a number of other radical organisations - *Preservation of the Rights of Prisoners (PROP), INQUEST, and Women in Prison* - who, implicitly or explicitly, adopted an abolitionist position around prisons. What united, (and continues to unite) these groups was the recognition that the prison was a place for inflicting punishment, pain and trauma onto, and into, the lives of the confined (Ryan and Ward, 2013: 9).

These groups challenged the cosy relationship that prevailed between the state and liberal prison reform groups built on the mystifying discourse that prisons were not only inevitable but also existed to rehabilitate the confined. Instead, abolitionists emphasised, and, indeed demonstrated, that the everyday life of the prison, built on the often-feral occupational culture of prison officers, was underpinned by the deadening discourse of punitive degradation for the majority of prisoners. Utilising the marginalised, vilified voices of prisoners was central to the abolitionist critique as it attempted to challenge the state's capacity to construct a particular form of 'truth' around prison issues (Fitzgerald and Sim, 1982). This strategy was reinforced by a newly emerging group of critical lawyers who exploited the contradictions in bourgeois law to enhance the few rights that prisoners were allowed in the appalling conditions that prevailed in the short-term prisons and the **psychological misery generated in the** 'electronic coffin[s]' of the long-term, maximum security prisons (King and Elliot, 1977: 3).

There were two significant, material and ideological outcomes from these overtly political interventions. First, they impacted on penal policy: the prison medical service was abolished; deaths in custody became visible; the role of coroners in marginalising the experiences of the families of the dead were highlighted; and the appalling treatment of women in prison were made apparent. Second, abolitionist groups had a hegemonic impact on more traditional liberal reform groups dragging them, sometimes reluctantly, onto a more radical political terrain, particularly in the area of deaths in custody (Sim, 2009). Over four decades on, and with this interventionist history in mind, what are the challenges that face contemporary abolitionists in the present neoliberal conjuncture faced, as we are, with the brutal onslaught on the economic, political and cultural institutions that came with the post-war settlement?   There are three issues I want to highlight.

Expanding The Penal

First, Justin Piche and Mike Larsen have argued that the impact of globalised, neoliberal economic policies, and the other insidious political processes that have followed including 'industrialised insecurity' and mass surveillance, has facilitated the emergence of a range of institutions, often privately operated, to detain, punish, and degrade the poor and the powerless. Thus, abolitionists need to expand the definition of 'what is to be abolished' and to think in terms of '*carceral* abolition' rather than simply prison abolition thereby addressing 'the use of confinement, and the systematic deprivation of liberty in spaces outside and adjacent to the penal system, as traditionally conceived' (Piche and Larsen, 2010: 392 and 398, emphasis in the original). Immigration removal centres based on incapacitation, exclusion and punitive coercion, provide a compelling example of Piche and Larsen's argument as well as illustrating the traumas experienced by those detained, both adults and children, held within them.   Between 1989 and 2014, the punitive environment in these institutions generated 21 deaths, with five further deaths being recorded between 2005 and 2014, not long after the detainees had been released (Athwal, 2014). Additionally, according to Women for Refugee Women, one in five of the women surveyed who had claimed asylum, and had been detained, had tried to kill themselves (Walter, 2014).

Punishing the Contemporary 'Rabble' in an Expanding Penal/Welfare Network

Second, there is the question of the coercive and destructive intertwining of penal and welfare institutions, propelled forward by private and third sector interests. The poor, endlessly and pitilessly, socially constructed as feckless scroungers, means that they are now surveilled and punished:

> *to a point where even Jeremy Bentham might have had misgivings. Any potential for deviance, including welfare deviance, is increasingly being ruthlessly suppressed, a coercive strategy legitimated by the cod-psychology articulated by a range of "judges of normality" (Foucault, 1979: 304) employed by both the state and private companies who are remorseless in their intent to psychologically break down welfare claimants and rebuild their 'deviant' personalities so that they become remoralised drones operating in the service economy*
> (Sim, 2014: 18)

The poor are not to be trusted. However, the self-surveilling rich *can* be trusted to act responsibly for the greater good of the wider social collective, despite *their* lamentable track record of feckless incompetence and brutal inefficiency exemplified in the financial crisis in 2008, and its aftermath. The final indignity in the attempt to induce respectable conformity is to expose poor families to the 'wisdom' of celebrities who offer them sage advice on how to manage their meagre budgets. In August 2009, Channel 4 exemplified this trend in *Benefit Busters*. The first programme centred on 'benefit buster', and **Action for Employment** (A4e) employee Hayley Taylor, whose job was:

> *to persuade single mothers on benefits to go back to work. The company she works for, A4e, which is helping to tackle the Government's target of getting 70 per cent of lone parents into paid work by 2010, is the largest welfare reform company in the world. A4e is run by multimillionaire entrepreneur Emma Harrison, who believes her business is "improving people's lives by getting them into work." Until*

recently, the 700,000 lone parents receiving benefit didn't have to look for work until their youngest child was 16. Soon, they must either work, or be looking for work, once their youngest child is seven. At Doncaster A4e, Hayley runs a course called Elevate that aims to give lone parents the skills and confidence to enter the workplace and convince them they'll be better off doing so. Cameras follow her group of ten single mothers during their intensive six-week course to prepare them for work. (www.channel4.com)

A4e was established at the end of the 1980s in Sheffield at a time when the steel industry was being decimated. By 2009, amongst its partners were Her Majesty's Prison Service, Crime Concern, the Criminal Records Office, NACRO, and the Universities of Hull, Edinburgh and Manchester Metropolitan. (A4E, n.d.). Harrison was awarded a CBE for 'services to unemployed people' in the 2009 New Year Honours list. The former Home Secretary David Blunkett was an advisor to the company while Sir Robin Young, the former permanent secretary at the Department of Trade and Industry was on the its board (Private Eye, 2010: 8). In the same year, A4e secured a five-year £800 million contract to run the Flexible New Deal scheme. This scheme was less concerned with forcing benefits claimants to write CVs and practice interview skills. Rather, 'A4e's "personal career coaches" are left to help "customers" devise a plan that can include a range of actions from community work and numeracy training through to getting people in remote areas on to mopeds, *and giving personal hygiene advice*' (The Guardian, 2010, emphasis added).

Yet the impact of changes to the benefits system has been devastating. In January 2013, in a Parliamentary debate, Michael Meacher MP noted, 'according to the Government's own figures... 1,300 persons [died] after being put into the work-related activity group, 2,200 people [died] before their assessment [was] complete, and 7,100 people [died] after being put into the support group...'(Hansard, 17 January 2013: col. 1051). For Rebecca Bohrman and Naomi Murakawa, the importance of this intertwining network of penal and welfare power is clear: 'welfare retrenchment and punishment expansion represent opposite trends in state spending but they rely on the same ideology. That ideology holds that the liberal welfare state corrodes personal responsibility, divorces work from reward, and lets crime go without punishment; consequently the lenient welfare regime attracts opportunistic immigrants and cultivates criminal values' (cited in Meiners, 2011: 21).

The 'Rehabilitation Revolution' and the Consolidation of State Power

Third, different political parties, of whatever political persuasion, have continued to maintain that the prison is a natural and necessary bulwark in maintaining law and order - whose law and what order that might be is not part of this debate. In Britain, the present Coalition government has proclaimed that a 'rehabilitation revolution' is taking place in prisons. This contention begs a number of questions: it ignores the fact that the prison remains a place of punishment, pain and violence; it fails to recognise that, given their social and economic marginalisation, prisoners have never been 'habitated' and so they 'have nothing to which they can be advantageously rehabilitated' (Carlen, cited in Cooper and Sim, 2013: 202); finally, this 'rehabilitation revolution' is being propelled forward by a range of private third sector and charitable organisations who are developing partnership programmes inside prisons for the confined. Significantly, this development has been socially constructed as the state losing its power and that this power is being dispersed across these organisations. Crucially, however, politically and theoretically, this development does *not* mean that the state is losing its power to punish. Instead, these partnerships are augmenting and reinforcing the power of the state and its institutions (Davies, 2011). Across a range of criminal justice institutions, not only prisons, the state is becoming *more*, not *less*, powerful: more intrusive, more repressive and more punitively interventionist into the lives of those increasingly marooned at the bottom of the neoliberal hierarchy of power and powerlessness (Sim,

2009). Therefore, critically considering the new configurations of state power is another issue for abolitionists to consider in the twenty first century.

Conclusion: Contesting Neoliberal Confinement

Building on the theoretical, political and interventionist work conducted by abolitionists over the last four decades, a number of writers have elaborated on the insights offered by this original work. Stephen Hartnett (2011: 3), for example, has argued that 'abolishing the prison-industrial complex should be at the head of a new human rights agenda for the twenty first century'. According to Justin Piche and Mike Larsen, abolitionists need to acknowledge 'new trends in confinement and to the linkages between them...it also requires the appreciation of the relationships between local struggles and practices, and global patterns' (Piche and Larsen, 2010: 405). For others, building on the concept of 'abolitionist alternatives' developed by Angela Davis (Davis, 2003: 109), there have been a number of policies developed in the UK, such as the Barlinnie Special Unit and Grendon Underwood, that are worth defending and which provide a glimpse of an abolitionist future (Sim 2009). Finally, for Erica Meiners, the economic, political and ideological power of neoliberalism is not totally determining. Put simply, 'we still have political agency' (Meiners, 2011: 33). This important point underscores the three concluding remarks I want to make.

First, despite what appears to be the omnipotent and omniscient hegemonic power of the state, that power network is often undermined by the contradictions, contingencies and contestable spaces that exist within, and between, its different institutions. As Hall et al have noted, 'hegemonies are never completed projects: they are always in contention. There are always cracks and contradictions - and therefore opportunities' (Hall et al, 2013: 20). In that sense, history is not on the side of the prison or the other penal institutions that have materialised in recent years. Struggles around these institutions are winnable, as abolitionists in England and Wales have demonstrated in the last four decades.

Second, and, allied to the above, it is important to recognise that there is a crisis of hegemony confronting the state in England and Wales.   This crisis is also a *moral* crisis in that the nefarious activities of state servants, particularly the police, have been highlighted across a range of different areas – misleading crime statistics, misleading welfare statistics, 'Plebgate', Hillsborough, phone hacking, the relentless surveillance of a range of groups involved in peaceful protest, the infiltration of the Stephen Lawrence campaign and other campaigning groups, assuming the identities of dead children and the hacking of Milly Dowler's phone after she was murdered.   These profoundly anti-democratic activities, many of which are illegal, have generated a deep moral and political crisis for the state. Abolitionism is not only concerned with political praxis but it is also a moral philosophy so in that sense the liberal discourse which constructs the state as the high point of moral reasoning and behaviour, is, as these activities illustrate, immensely problematic and, in turn, opens up a space for thinking about radically different social and criminal justice polices and, by extension, a better world.

Third, it is also important for abolitionism to maintain the ongoing critique of reformism and retain its sense of utopianism about displacing punishment.   The modern prison is the reformed prison, a process which, as Foucault has noted, has been ongoing (and unravelling) for the last two centuries.   What is required, as Russell Jacoby has argued, is to get beyond dichotomising the discourses of reform and utopianism (or, in this case, abolitionism) so that:

> the choice we have is not between reasonable proposals and an unreasonable utopianism. Utopian thinking does not undermine or discount real reforms.   Indeed, it is almost the opposite; **practical reforms depend on utopian dreaming - or at least utopian thinking drives incremental improvements.**
> (Jacoby, cited in Sim, 2009: 162, emphasis added)

In conclusion, the strategy for making abolitionist interventions involves identifying the 'cracks, the silent tremors and dysfunctions in....institutions' (Foucault, 2002: 458). In doing so, it is possible to make an inch of difference to the exercise of power both inside and outside of the prison walls. As the great American writer James Baldwin once noted, 'the world changes according to the way people see it, and if you alter even by a millimetre the way people look at reality, then you can change it' (cited in Truth Out, n.d.). Baldwin's eloquent, empowering prose perfectly encapsulates the ethical vision beating righteously within the collective hearts of abolitionists. It is a vision which, despite the deadly spiritual and material corrosion engendered by neoliberalism, can still turn heads and transform aspiring possibilities into political probabilities.

References

Athwal, H. (2014) *Deaths in Immigration Detention 1989-2014* London: Institute of Race Relations.

Cooper, V. and Sim, J. (2013) *Punishing the detritus and the dammed: penal and semi-penal institutions in Liverpool and the North West* in Scott, D. (ed) Why Prison? Cambridge: Cambridge University Press.

Davis, A. (2003) *Are Prisons Obsolete?* New York: Seven Sisters Press.

Davies, J. (2011) *Challenging Governance Theory* Bristol: Policy Press.

Fitzgerald, M. and Sim, J. (1982) *British Prisons* Oxford: Blackwell.

Foucault, M. (1979) *Discipline and Punish* Harmondsworth: Penguin.

Foucault, M. (2002) *Power: Essential Works of Foucault 1954-1984 Vol. 3* (edited by Faubion, J.) London: Penguin

Hall, S. (1988) *The Hard Road to Renewal* London: Verso.

Hall, S., Massey, D. and Rustin, M. (2013) *After neoliberalism: analysing the present* in Soundings Issue 53, Spring: 8-22.

Truth-Out   (N.D.)   available   at   http://truth-out.org/news/item/14814-the-politics-of-disimagination-and-the-pathologies-of-power Accessed 16 March 2013.

King, R. and Elliott. K. (1977) *Albany: birth of a prison, end of an era* London: Routledge

Meiners. E. R. (2011) *Building an Abolition Democracy; or, The Fight Against Public Fear, Private Benefits and Prison Expansion* in Hartnett, S. J. (ed) Challenging the Prison Industrial Complex Urbana: University of Illinois Press.

Panitch, L. and Leys, C. (2005) *Preface* in Panitch, L. and Leys, C. (eds) The Socialist Register 2006 London: The Merlin Press.

Piche, J. and Larsen, M. (2010*) The moving targets of penal abolitionism: ICOPA, past, present and future* in Contemporary Justice Review: Issues in Criminal, Social and Restorative Justice, 13, 4: 391-410.

Ryan, M. and Ward, T. (2013) *Prison Abolition in the UK; They Dare Not Speak Its Name* (Unpublished paper, available from the authors).

Sim, J. (2009) *Punishment and Prisons* London: Sage

Sim, J. (2014) *'"Welcome to the Machine": Poverty and Punishment in Austere Times'* in Prison Service Journal Vol: 123:17-23.

Walter, N. (2014) *Margaret's Story: raped in Congo, locked up in UK* in The Guardian 10th June: 12-13.

CHAPTER 7:

Playing The Get Out Of Jail For Free Card: Creating A New 'Abolitionist Consensus'?

David Scott

> *... whenever experiences shows that certain things do not answer the purpose for which they were intended, then the right to continue ceases. That is, whenever it becomes apparent that certain acts done for the purposes of punishment do not serve the purposes for which they were intended - i.e. do not tend to protect society - then the right to repeat them ceases, and any further repetition of them will be simply a wrong done by society to one of its members, an injury inflicted by the strong on the weak.*

So wrote John Peter Altgeld (1884:50) 130 years ago in his book *Our Penal Machinery and its Victims*. In this classic text Altgeld raised major objections to the imprisonment of children, women and the use of remand, and his critique of the 'penal machinery' is all the more interesting because at time of writing he was a serving American Judge. Previous papers have pointed to numerous limitations facing contemporary sites of confinement, indicating that time has once again come to recognise, as Altgeld did, that their repetition is 'simply a wrong done by society' by the 'strong on the weak'.

The case against prisons 'right to continue' (Ibid) seems all the more pertinent in our time of 'hyper-incarceration' (Wacquant, 2010). Indeed the recent growth in the Average Daily Population (ADP) of prisoners in England and Wales is staggering. At the end of 1992, for example, the ADP stood at around 40,600 prisoners, yet by October 2011 the daily population had surpassed 88,000. Although the ADP has declined in recent months – on Friday 22nd March 2013 there were 84,501 people in prisons and young offender institutions in England and Wales and a further 366 children held in secure children's homes and secure training centres - prisoner populations are out of control.   Despite such exponential growth it remains all too clear that prison does not work, at least when measured against its official aims (Sim, 2009). 47% of adults are reconvicted within one year of release. This figure increases to 60% for ex-prisoners who served sentences of less than 12 months and to as high as 70% for those who have served more than ten prison sentences (MoJ, 2009).

When challenging hyper-incarceration, abolitionists must advocate strategies and tactics that can be adopted in our historical conjuncture and thus be immediately influential. This should not mean compromising abolitionist values or abandoning utopian visions or radical alternatives, but rather being politically astute and having a clear strategy of engagement.   The most important question, I think, for penal abolitionists today is 'what can we do right now to challenge hyper-incarceration and yet at the same time leave open the possibility for radical change?'

Our escape from hyper-incarceration begins by reversing the tide and making small steps towards penal abolition and the creation of a society rooted in the principles of social justice and acknowledgement of common humanity.   Any successful intervention must be abolitionist, for it is only by adopting abolitionist principles and values that we can hope to avoid 'co-option' (Mathiesen, 1974) and 'carceral clawback' (Carlen, 2002).   Yet abolitionists cannot achieve this alone. We need a broad based alliance that draws upon penal pressure groups, the liberal penal lobby - penal minimalists, reductionists and moderates – as well as progressive politicians, practitioners and members of the general public. Further, both penal and social transformation can only be achieved through alliances with other radical social movements committed to social justice, anti-violence and human dignity for all. We need a counter-hegemonic strategy and consensus consistent with abolitionist values and sensibilities if we are to effectively dismantle the penal apparatus of the Capitalist state.

I have referred elsewhere to how an abolitionist real utopia (Scott, 2013a, 2013b) would aim to challenge hyper-incarceration whilst at the same time promote radical social and penal transformation. Such an abolitionist real utopia would be grounded within the immanent real world conditions of our historical moment and its strategy for the radical reduction in prison populations would draw upon the 'attrition model' and its associated stance of the 'selective abolition'. Let us consider this further.

The writings of John Peter Altgeld and William Nagel both espoused embryonic versions of the attrition model, but it is the writings of Faye Honey Knopp and colleagues in their abolitionist handbook *Instead of Prisons,* first published in 1976, that laid down the principles of this approach. In short, the attrition model aims to gradually reduce imprisonment:

> *'Attrition' which means the rubbing away or wearing down by friction, reflects the **persistent and continuing** strategy necessary to diminish the function and power of prisons in our society.*
> (Knopp, 1976: 62, emphasis in original)

In the last thirty five and more years the attrition model has been promoted by abolitionists such as Thomas Mathiesen, Stanley Cohen, Joe Sim and Julia Oparah and I believe it remains one of the most plausible abolitionist strategies yet devised. The associated model of selective abolitionism, which has been advocated by abolitionists such as Pat Carlen, Phil Scraton, Barbara Hudson, Barry Goldson and Deb Coles, is rooted in the assumption that certain categories of lawbreakers must not be sent to prison because of (1) the relative harmlessness of the offence, (2) the vulnerabilities of the person who has broken the law, or (3) that imprisonment has unnecessarily harmful consequences that should, if at all possible, be avoided. Such lawbreakers, albeit perhaps on different grounds, should be deliberately excluded from imprisonment. Alongside Helen Codd, I brought a number of these grouping of prisoners together to present a holistic case for selective abolitionism in our book *Controversial Issues in Prisons* (Scott & Codd, 2010). Here it was maintained that selective abolitionism could be immediately adopted by politicians and penal campaigners who wished to lobby the government for major reductions in the prison population.

It was recognised that such an approach must be conscious of the contradictions and the dangers generated by this strategy. Attrition and selective abolitionism are not enough on their own. They must be understood as part of a wider abolitionist critiques of prisons and criminal processes and as the first steps on a path to a socially just society. On this assumption, I believe the seven well debated 'tactics' detailed below may lead us in the right direction and help generate a new abolitionist based consensus. Collectively they entail, to use a metaphor from the popular board game *Monopoly*, playing the 'get out of jail for free' card.

1. Moratorium on all prison building

I would like to suggest that an anti-prison activist's first priority should be to organise international, national and local campaigns challenging the moral, economic and political viability of building more prisons. Indeed, stopping the building of new prisons is essential for the success of penal reduction. Moratoriums directly challenge the prison building programmes and are a crucial intervention for the following eight reasons:

i)   There is recognition that the level of financial investment in prison building deters politicians from later calling for penal reduction.

ii) It provides an opportunity to draw attention to the direct costs of penal incarceration and may allow some discussion of its hidden costs – both human and financial.

iii) It recognises that the inherent harms and pains of penal incarceration cannot be removed by improved physical conditions.

iv) It can facilitate discussion of how money allocated to prison building could be reinvested in new employment possibilities in the community which do not deliberately inflict pain on other humans.

v)   Political pressure is created to develop alternative policies and indicates to politicians that they can no longer simply expand the penal apparatus to deal with pressing social problems.

vi) It directly challenges privatization and companies such as Serco and G4S that build prisons, focusing attention on the limitations of private finance initiatives and engendering support by penal practitioners and the liberal penal lobby opposed to privatisation.

vii) It provides a focussed campaign against new prisons and there is a strong possibility that such an intervention could generate new alliances.

viii) It is something that can be achieved in our historic conjuncture. In the current economic climate economic expenditure is clearly an area of vulnerability and one that can be exploited.

2. Targeting existing prisons for immediate closure

A moratorium may help to create the political will to do something about our high prison populations, and this can be enhanced by calls to close existing prisons (Sim, 2009). Lists of the 'worst prisons' can be drawn up in a number of different ways, but perhaps the greatest immediate influence comes from those prisons highlighted in 'official discourse' such a reports from Her Majesty's Chief Inspectors of Prisons [HMCIP]. On such a basis, the following three prisons could be earmarked for immediate closure:

i)   HMP Wandsworth, has recently been described by the *Guardian* (13, March, 2013) as "Britain's worst jail". A 2011 HMCIP report highlights how the prison was 'demeaning, unsafe and indecent' where some prisoners were kept locked up for 22 hours day whilst others had no access to showers for months on end.   An authoritarian officer culture pertained and there were serious concerns about 'unnecessary and disproportionate' prison officer violence. In March 2013 HMP Wandsworth was the fourth most overcrowded jail, exceeding capacity by 448 prisoners (167% over capacity).

ii)   The third most overcrowded prison in England and Wales in March 2013 was HMP Lincoln, which was 170% over capacity.   In the December 2011 report the HMCIP found Lincoln prison 'unsafe' with unacceptable levels of bullying, victimisation and assaults. Prisoners lived in 'filthy conditions' and were kept locked up for most of the day.   Prison officers appeared morally indifferent to the painful realities of prisoners.

iii) In a damning HMCIP report from July 2010 HMP Dartmoor was described as having a "pervasive negative culture" grounded in the antiquated principles of less eligibility. Dartmoor prison was unsafe, violent and there was strong evidence of prison officer racism, homophobia and other forms discrimination.

The Prison Service in England and Wales has closed 13 prisons in the last four years, with seven prisons closed in March 2013 - Bullwood Hall; Camp Hill; Canterbury; Gloucester; Kingston; Shepton Mallet; Somerset; and Shrewsbury. Abolitionists need to call for similar clusters of closures without new prisons being opened (Sim, 2009). In the first instance, the targeting of the 'worst prisons' (with recognition that there may well be much worse jails than Wandsworth) may prove most persuasive to penal authorities and gain support from other constituents in the penal lobby.

3. Virtual end of remands in custody

The prison has been a place of custody holding people awaiting trial for more than 1,000 years (Pugh, 1968). In

March 2013 there were 13,000 people in prison on remand. The limitations of pre-trial / preventive detention have been long identified, and have been central to the liberal penal lobby in the UK since at least the publication of *A Taste of Prison* (King and Morgan, 1976) some 37 years ago. Remand prisoners today continue to face significant difficulties, including experiencing more impoverished living conditions than sentenced prisoners (HMCIP, 2012). People on remand have less access to facilities, basic 'entitlements' and preparations for their legal proceedings are likely to be greatly inhibited. Each year 29,400 people remanded in custody are not given a prison sentence (Ibid). It is now widely recognised that remand is not necessary to ensure a person's return to court for trial (Ibid). One way therefore of immediately reducing the prison population is to abolish pre-trial detention for all but the very small number of accused that genuinely present a threat to public safety. Such an initiative could reduce the prison population by around 10,000 in as little as three months.

4. **Decriminalisation of 'victimless'/'harmless' acts**

One way to 'reduce the flow' of people into prison is to stop imprisoning individuals that have undertaken 'victimless' or 'harmless' petty offences. I will briefly consider substance users and drug takers here. Abolitionists have argued that it is important to suspend our judgement on drug taking, arguing that whether we morally approve of them or not, such victimless acts cannot be effectively regulated by the criminal law (Knopp, 1976). There are estimated to be more than 400,000 illegal drug-users in the United Kingdom (Seddon, 2006) and over 250,000 drug takers have been officially defined as 'problematic drug users' [PDU's]. It is estimated that 75,000 PDU's pass through the prison system annually and that 45,000 PDU's are currently in prison (NOMS, 2005). Prisons are designed to contain, punish and deliver blame through pain rather than facilitate the care or positive transformation of individuals. In Portugal drug taking and the possession of drugs has been decriminalised and drug problems are now considered a public health issue. Money that would have been spent on penal incarceration is spent on health care, which is around 75% cheaper than the previous penal strategy. As a result there has been both a reduction in heroin usage and in drug-related property offences in Portugal. Extensive evidence from the UK suggests that treatments of drug takers are more likely to be successful in the community than through criminal justice interventions (Bennett and Holloway, 2005). This implies that if treatment is a genuine aspiration it would be more sensible to decriminalise drug taking (Scott and Codd, 2010). Adoption of a public health agenda for drug taking would reduce the prison population by tens of thousands in a very short period of time.

5. Raise the age of criminal responsibility

Criminal processes in the main control and regulate the behaviour of children and young adults. Official data indicate that lawbreakers reach peaks in offending rates in the mid teens - although such data can and should be problematised as it is based on officially recorded 'crimes' and negates much adult crime undertaken in private spaces. Penal custody seems grossly inappropriate for children and young adults, for they are unlikely to have the life experience or coping skills required to deal with either punitive environments or the loss of close personal relationships. Most children imprisoned are not persistent offenders - with many having only one or two previous offences - and are most likely to have committed petty property offences. Imprisoned children are characterised by poverty, family instability, emotional, physical and sexual abuse, homelessness, isolation, loneliness, self-harm and disadvantage (Goldson, 2005; Goldson and Coles, 2005). Many children in custody have learning difficulties; been placed on the child protection registry; have self harmed in the past; and have grown up in state care homes. Raising the age of criminal responsibility to initially 14 and the later to 16 would allow for alternative ways of dealing with children in trouble to come to prominence. For those people under the age of 18 the courts should be asked to restrict interventions to police warnings, suspended sentences or unconditional discharges and thus de-naturalise the idea that confinement is suitable for any child.   Human rights and children's charities would be natural allies and would broaden the basis of an abolitionist consensus.

6. Diversion of vulnerable people from criminal processes

There are a number of people with vulnerabilities imprisoned today that should be diverted from the criminal process, but here I focus exclusively upon people with mental health problems.   Mental health problems are often linked with homelessness, poverty and unemployment, and *The Social Exclusion Report* (2002, cited in Scott, 2008: 116) notes that

- 80% of prisoners have mental health problems (66,000 people)
- 20% of male and 15% of female sentenced prisoners have previously been admitted to a mental hospital
- 95% of young prisoners aged 15 to 21 suffer from a mental health problem.

Prolonged passivity leads to isolation and the prison place presents a serious danger to the mental health of those confined. Numerous aspects of the daily prison regime are potentially damaging: crowding; frustrations dealing with the minuet of everyday life; lack of mental or physical stimulation; the preponderance of negative relationships rooted in fear, anxiety and mistrust; physical, emotional, sexual or financial exploitation; and inadequate care with an over-emphasis on medication (Scott and Codd, 2010).

Political momentum for the diversion of people with mental health problems reached a new crescendo as recently as March 2011, when the then Justice Secretary Ken Clarke called for enhanced diversion schemes.   There are currently over 100 adult Criminal Justice Liaison and Diversion schemes (established 1999) in England which assess and advise on mental health needs of offenders, sometimes referring offenders for treatment rather than punishment.

From April 2013, Health and Wellbeing Boards will commission health and social care services, including those with mental health problems. Abolitionists should try and influence the new Health and Wellbeing Boards to enhance provision for diversion. Whilst conscious of the problems of 'net widening' (Cohen, 1985) and recognition that detention in a mental health institution may be just as problematic as being confined in a penal one, highlighting the inappropriateness of punishing people with mental health problems could mean that tens of thousands of people are diverted from prison.

7. Decarceration of people from custody who have undertaken relatively harmless acts

Finally we turn to the immediate removal people from prison. As detailed above, there are number of prisoners with vulnerabilities that have undertaken relatively harmless acts, but I will focus here only on women prisoners as an illustrative example. Over a third of all adult women in prison have no previous convictions, and most women sentenced to imprisonment are sentenced for non-violent offences, with the largest group being sentenced for drug offences (Ministry of Justice 2008). The numbers of women prisoners has slightly fallen in recent times and on the 22nd March 2013 there were 3,968 women in prison. Women are not imprisoned for the seriousness of the act perpetrated, but rather because of *who* they are: women who do not conform to a particular expectation of womanhood are those most likely to find themselves in prison (Scott and Codd, 2010). Most women offenders are not dangerous and approximately 3,000 of the women in prison could be released in a matter of weeks via early release; probation; home monitoring; and amnesties. Sentencers could also pilot the introduction of waiting lists for women offenders.

Not only, but also...

The above seven tactics are well rehearsed and many are shared across the political spectrum of the penal lobby but from an abolitionist perspective it is crucial that they are not deployed in isolation of wider critiques of criminal processes, punishment or introduction of social reforms rooted in social justice. Abolitionists must constantly guard against the possibility of arguments of the attrition model / selective abolition being co-opted or used to justify the responsibilisation of offenders and subsequent negation of their care post-release (Hannah-Moffat, 2001). Abolitionists must also ensure that this strategy is not used to obfuscate the inherent harms and pains of imprisonment. The concern can perhaps be best illustrated through a consideration of 'suicidal ideation'. Prisons are deadly. In 2013 more than one prisoner took their own life every week in prisons in England and Wales and the likelihood of a prisoner taking their own life is between four and eleven times higher than the general population (Scott and Codd, 2010). Coping is a tenuous, relative and fluid concept that ebbs and flows over time. Somewhere between one third and one half of the prison population have suicidal thoughts, and many have recently thought about taking their lives. If such figures are accurate this would involve somewhere in the region of 42,000 people (Ibid). The prison place is a toxic environment and all humans placed in such a degrading and damaging place are vulnerable to its structured harms. Abolitionists must therefore continue to question the core assumptions of the penal rationale and not focus exclusively upon prisoners who can most easily be defined as 'vulnerable', whatever its political utility.

Abolitionists recognise that the law reflects the interests of those who hold power rather than upholding a widely accepted moral code. Most people are regular law breakers yet most 'criminal acts' are not penalised. For every 100 serious crimes reported, 25 people are arrested, 12 are convicted and three end up in prison (Knopp, 1976). Those that are imprisoned are disproportionately from working class, poor and impoverished social backgrounds (Sim, 2009). Abolitionists must keep at the forefront of the debate the problems of economic and social inequalities and strive to develop of alliances with social movements promoting human rights and social justice. Undoubtedly we must, somehow, try to create a new 'abolitionist consensus' that can make a

IVERPOOL JOHN MOORES UNIVERSITY
LEARNING SERVICES

difference here and now. Yet at the same time abolitionists and anti-prison activists must also continue to aspire to live in, and fight for, a *world without prisons.*

References

Altgeld, J.P. (1884) *Our penal machinery and its victims* New York: A. C. McClurg

Bennett, T. and Holloway, K. (2005) *Understanding drugs, alcohol and crime* Berkshire: Open University Press

Carlen, P. (2002*) 'End of Award Report: Funding Report ECHR: L216252033 ECHR'* Unpublished Document

Cohen, S. (1985) *Visions of Social Control* Cambridge: Polity Press

Goldson, B. (2005) 'Child Imprisonment: A Case for Abolition', *Youth Justice* Vol. 5 No.2, pp.77-90.

Goldson, B. and Coles, D. (2005) *In the care of the state?* London: INQUEST

Hannah-Moffat, K. (2001) *Punishment in Disguise* Toronto: University of Toronto Press

HMCIP (2010) *Inspection of HMP Dartmouth* London: HMCIP

HMCIP (2011a) *Inspection of HMP Wandsworth* London: HMCIP

HMCIP (2011b) *Inspection of HMP Lincoln* London: HMCIP

HMCIP (2012) *Thematic Review on Remand Prisoners* London: HMCIP

King, R. and Morgan, R. (1976) *A Taste of Prison* London: RKP

Knopp, F.H. (1976) *Instead of Prisons* California: Critical Resistance

Mathiesen, T. (1974) *The Politics of Abolition* Oxford: Martin Robertson

Ministry of Justice [MoJ] (2008) *Offender Management Caseload Statistics 2008*, London: The Stationery Office.

Ministry of Justice [MoJ] (2009) *Re-offending of adults: results from the 2007 cohort* London: The Stationery Office

National Offender Management Service [NOMS] (2005) *Strategy for the management and treatment of drug users within the correctional services* London: NOMS

Pugh, R.B. (1968) *Imprisonment in medieval England* Cambridge: Cambridge University Press

Scott, D. (2008) *Penology* London: Sage

Scott, D. (2013a) "Visualising and abolitionist real utopia: principles, policy and praxis" in Malloch, M. & Munro, W. (eds) *Crime, Critique and Utopia* London: Palgrave

Scott, D. (2013b) "Unequalled in pain" in Scott, D. (ed) *Why Prison?* Cambridge: Cambridge University Press

Scott, D. & Codd, H. (2010) *Controversial Issues in Prisons* Buckingham: Open University Press

Seddon, T. (2006) "Drugs, crime and social exclusion: social context and social theory in British drugs-crime research" in *British Journal of Criminology* Volume 46, No. 4 pp 680-703

Sim, J. (2009) *Punishment and Prisons* London: Sage

Wacquant, L. (2010), 'Class, race and hyper-incarceration in revanchist America', *Daedalus*, 139 (3), Summer 2010, pp 70–80

CONCLUSION

Victoria Canning

This collection has sought to draw attention to the challenges faced through various sites of confinement – detention, imprisonment and in restrictive and restraining systems or procedures. Although disparate in the specific focusses of each chapter, the contributions have highlighted many issues facing contemporary debates, including the challenges faced in relation to penal policy, social control and populist punitiveness. From the offset, the rolling back of state responsibility is critically addressed, and as Bell argues, the simultaneous rolling forward of – often harmful - social control agendas has serious consequences for the lives of powerless populations. The example given may be politically and culturally specific to contemporary neoliberal Britain, but the key concerns certainly resonate with wider critical criminological literatures working across other parts of the globe.

The implications for those at the socio-economic 'bottom of the heap' (King, 2012) are evidenced in Cooper's research around women's lives in semi-penal institutions. Although not claiming neoliberalism is singularly responsible for many of the issues arising, the case studies do highlight the impacts of so-called austerity measures in some ways, such as cutbacks on services and support. Crucially, however, the intensification of gendered controls by the state in women offenders' personal lives is made clear. The issues discussed by Cooper in some ways expand on what is meant by confinement, not only spatially but through the dissolution of autonomy and community networks through mismanaged dispersal strategies. Women's lives are literally absorbed into a system that moves them from established networks to areas far outside their background communities, reiterating wider arguments long made by feminist working in the fields of gendered geographies of punishment (Barton, 2005; Carlen, 1990; Pallot and Piacentini, 2012).

Chapter Two thus alludes to ways in which women cope with living in or between semi-penal institutions. This theme of coping, or more specifically survival, is drawn out by Jefferson in Chapter Three in relation to political protest groups and Muslim detainees. As he argues in the first instance, studies of prison outside of Western contexts are relatively rare in European criminologies. The voices resonate with wider findings from prison ethnographies – a yearning for family life, for time to pass and ultimately for freedom to come (Drake et al, 2015; Sim, 1990; Stevens, 2012.).

These forms of confinement – temporal and physical – set a backdrop for the following two chapters looking at 'crimmigration' (Stumpf, 2006) and immigration detention. They each draw out the impacts of two forms of incarceration – physical, as experienced by John (Chapter Four) through his imprisonment, and temporal, as in the insidious control of asylum seekers' lives through a dual process of producing and implementing structurally harmful policies and practice, whilst denying or overlooking much needed psycho-social support. As legal practitioners and criminologists have argued elsewhere (Bosworth, 2008; Canning, 2014; Webber, 2012), the lives of asylum seekers may be indefinitely suspended through long application procedures and decision making processes, as well as through immigration detention and the criminalisation of migrant bodies. Bhatia and Cockcroft elucidate the limitations of detention in this way and, importantly, the impacts that both temporal and physical confinement can have on the individuals caught in a structurally flawed and punitive system originally intended to support individuals fleeing poverty and persecution (Webber, 2012).

Two key themes continue from these chapters through to Sim's abolitionist argument in Chapter Six. Firstly, like the work undertaken by Bhatia and Cockcroft, Sim emphasises the value of 'utilising the marginalised, vilified voices of prisoners' (this volume), an approach that has been central to both critical criminology and, beyond prison research, radical feminism. It is this that offers an alternative perspective of life in confinement. Secondly, Chapter Six advances previous points made throughout the collection by specifically addressing the broader question of punishment and its relationship with welfare networks and private sector interests. state power, Sim argues, is manifest well beyond the prison, embedded in and through cultural practices and institutions that earlier critical thinkers could not have anticipated.

As Scott points out in Chapter Seven, abolitionist thinkers (and arguably critical social sciences more generally) have long set the human at the centre of their study. While the number of people imprisoned is central to challenging hyper-incarceration, when we move beyond abstract (at times even unreliable) figures and look to the human cost of imprisonment, we allow ourselves scope to consider the harms that confinement can create (Carlton, 2007; Segrave and Carlton, 2011). Increases in mental health problems and high rates of recidivism, self-harm and suicide are evident in institutions globally. Disparities in the sentencing of poor populations, Black and Minority Ethnic Groups, refugees, and so-called 'deviant' women, suggests pervasive inequality and a need for fundamental restructuring of punishment and social control. It is with this in mind that the Prisons, Punishment and Detention Working Group put forward the following recommendations[1]:

Prisons, detention and punishment manifesto

I. An **international moratorium** on building new sites of confinement (prisons / asylums / immigration centres) and on the allocation of existing buildings and spaces as locations of involuntary detention;

II. An **end to the privatisation** of sites of confinement and the insidious expansion of the carceral state via the voluntary and private sector;

III. A detailed and critical interrogation of existing state detention, followed by a systematic call for governments to **close the most inhumane,**

[1] These recommendations are based in part on the arguments made by Scott (this volume) and adapted and agreed by the Prisons, Punishment and Detention Working Group steering committee in March 2013. See also Gilmore, J., Moore, J. and Scott, D. (2013) Critique and Dissent, Ottawa: Red Quill

degrading and torturous sites of confinement without opening new houses of detention;

IV.   A virtual **end to pre-trial detention** and the abolishment of the antiquated notion of bail except for those who present a serious threat to society;

V.   The safeguarding and **expansion of the legal rights of detainees**. Post incarceration ex-detainees must be recognised as full citizens and given full and uninhibited access to employment, housing, other social and financial services and full access to political and civil society;

VI.   The **decriminalisation of victimless and harmless acts**, such as alcoholism, deviant sexualities between consenting adults, substance misuse and drug taking. The criminalisation of sex workers (who are often from working class backgrounds) is harmful and victimising and we propose alternative responses that protect and prioritise the safety of the men and women who engage in this work;

VII.   The **decriminalisation of infringements of migration laws;**

VIII.   To **raise the age of criminal responsibility** in all countries in the world to the age of at least 16;

IX.   To **divert people with mental health problems, learning disabilities, severe physical disabilities, the profoundly deaf and people with suicidal ideation** from the criminal process whilst at the same time ensuring any alternative interventions are both 'in place' of a penal sanction and are not merely forms of 'trans-incarceration' to other sites of confinement;

X.   To immediately **remove those people most vulnerable to the inherent harms** and pains of confinement from places of detention;

XI.   To **formulate and advocate radical alternatives to the criminal process** and social injustices for individual and social harms that are feasible and could be implemented immediately or within a short period of time;

XII.   To propose that all governments **prioritise meeting human need, recognising common humanity and facilitating social justice** as the most effective means of preventing / dealing with human troubles, conflicts and problematic conduct.

References

Barton A. (2005), *'Fragile Moralities and Dangerous Sexualities: Two Centuries of Semi-Penal Institutionalisation for Women'*, Surrey: Ashgate

Bosworth, M. (2008) *Border Control and the Limits of the Sovereign State,* Social and Legal Studies Vol. 17: 199

Carlen, P. (1990) *Alternatives to Women's Imprisonment,* Milton Keynes: Open University Press, 1990

Carlton, B.A. (2007) *Imprisoning Resistance: Life and Death in an Australian Supermax,* Sydney Australia: Institute of Criminology Press

Drake, D. H., Earle, R. and Sloan, J. (2015) *International Handbook on Prison Ethnography.* Basingstoke: Palgrave (forthcoming)

King, R. H. (2012) *From the Bottom of the Heap,* Oakland: PM Press

Pallot, J. and Piacentini, L. (2012) *Gender, Geography and Punishment: The Experience of Women Prisoners in Carceral Russia,* Oxford: Oxford University Press

Segrave, M. and Carlton, B. (2011) *Counting the costs of imprisonment: researching women's post-release deaths in Victoria,* Australian and New Zealand Journal of Criminology, Vol. 44, Issue 1: p. 41-55

LIVERPOOL JOHN MOORES UNIVERSITY
LEARNING SERVICES

Sim, J. (1990) *Medical Power in Prisons: Prison Medical Service in England, 1774-1988* Buckingham: Open University Press

Stevens, A. (2012) *'I am the person now I was always meant to be': identity reconstruction and narrative reframing in therapeutic community prisons,* <u>Criminology and Criminal Justice,</u> Vol. 12, No. 5, p: 527-547

Stumpf, J.P. (2006) *The Crimmigration Crisis: Immigrants, Crime and Sovereign Power,* <u>American University Law Review</u>, Vol. 56

Webber, L. (2012) *Borderline Justice: The Fight for Refugee and Migrant Rights* London: Pluto Press

APPENDIX 1:

Conference report by Mark Hayes, Southampton Solent University, England

Conference: Sites of Confinement
Centre for the Study of Crime, Criminalisation and Social Exclusion
22 March 2013 Liverpool JMU

The above conference was used to launch the European Working Group on Prisons, Detention and Punishment, and was organised by Vicky Canning of Liverpool John Moores University. In fact, as a non-expert in this field, I saw attendance at this conference as an opportunity to learn something interesting about penal policy, incarceration and modes of confinement, rather than as an opportunity to contribute anything meaningful to the debates. Inevitably, therefore, my comments on the conference are impressionistic rather than analytical, and I apologise in advance for that. Nevertheless my thoughts may still provide other European Group members with a flavour of the event.

The first presentation was delivered by Emma Bell, who provided an excellent contextual overview of the neo-liberal framework within which penal policy has been constructed. This was important, of course, not only because practical policy outcomes cannot be detached from the ideological assumptions which currently prevail, but also because that particular ideological manifestation, "neo-liberalism", is almost entirely pernicious in its social consequences. The emphasis on specifically "neo-liberal" solutions has infected penal policy, and Emma Bell made this point with admirable clarity. In fact, listening to Emma I was reminded of an old joke: "how many neo-liberal free market economists does it take to change a lightbulb?" Of course the answer is *"none, because they all sit around waiting for the 'invisible hand'"*. Hayek, Friedman and the other disciples of unfettered free enterprise capitalism have an awful lot to answer for!

In the subsequent sessions Vickie Cooper examined semi-penal hostels, and made interesting observations about "punishment by dispersal", and Andrew Jefferson outlined an ambitious comparative research project which aims to assess prisons in Kosovo, Sierra Leone and the Philippines – research which will undoubtedly yield important empirical data. Monish Bhatia provided some extraordinary detail on the actual experience of asylum seekers and the social effect of the attempt to control "illegal" migration. Monish's prescient remarks were underscored by the contribution of Social Worker Eloise Cockcroft of *Revive*, an organisation which provides support and legal advice for those people seeking asylum. Eloise provided evidence to indicate quite clearly that the Border Agency is not "fit for purpose". In fact Eloise's eloquent presentation induced a variety of emotions and threw into a much sharper light the perverse priorities of a Coalition government which appears to know the price of everything and the value of nothing! Those members of the European Group anxious to discover more about this might consult the website of the National Coalition of Anti-Deportation Campaigns (NCADC). Here there is information on how to supply practical help to those individuals requiring assistance, two of whom (Fozia and Nawaz) related their story to conference members. The experience of Fozia and Nawaz was a potent reminder of the human cost of toxic social policies.

In the afternoon Joe Sim articulated a message that was not only witty and informative, but deliberate in its underlying purpose of speaking truth to power. The presentation, moreover, was delivered in undiluted working class Glaswegian mode – it bristled with righteous indignation and anger at the grotesque inequity, indeed the sheer absurdity, of contemporary penal policy (my partner is Glaswegian, so I know it doesn't pay to make them angry – I often have to sleep with one eye open!). I was left with two over-riding impressions after listening to Joe: firstly that the students at JMU are lucky to be taught by him; and secondly that it would be great to see him on Question Time with Theresa May! The latter prospect is unlikely of course, not least because Joe could deconstruct and destroy a Ministerial reputation in the time it takes to boil a kettle! Joe Sim is simply too dangerous for widespread public consumption.

Dave Scott ended the conference with a concise account of what needed to be done, and he set out a programme of action designed to engage activists with a shared agenda. It was a perfect way to finish because Dave embodies that synthesis of academic and activist which is so characteristic of the European Group. Dave Scott has the capacity to critically evaluate and conceptualise, as well as being able to plot a progressive path toward a better future via an emphasis on more sensible and socially responsible penal policy.

Overall the conference was successful because it facilitated a broad contextual analysis, it examined key areas of weakness in policy practice by focussing on specific examples, and it constructed a programme of action designed to address the difficulties that had been identified. This is precisely what committed, critically engaged academics in the social sciences should be doing. (However, if I was to make a single critical observation it would be that I would have thought Vicky Canning could have provided better weather! It was freezing, and I am certain that if Sam Fletcher was still at JMU she would have organised blinding sunshine!).

Mark Hayes
25 March 2013

APPENDIX 2:

European Group Resolutions Passed on 22nd March 2013:

Resolution against the excessive use of detention in the UK and across the globe

Members of the European Group for the Study of Deviance and Social Control would like to express their deep concern at the record high levels of detention in the United Kingdom in 2013. We believe that the number of people currently detained under immigration, mental health and penal law is unacceptable and presents a serious danger to democracy. We believe as academics, students, activists and members of the general public that it is important that a principled and practical stand is taken now against current expansionist penal policies and call upon the government of the United Kingdom to make immediate provision for a radical reduction in the number of people detained. Members of the European Group also offer their full support to activists and campaigners currently working to expose the brutal realities of detainment in the UK and elsewhere and offer our solidarity with their struggles for a more socially just society and the promotion of more humane means of dealing with problematic human conduct popularly referred to as 'crime'.

Resolution in support of the National Coalition of Anti-Deportation Campaigns and similar activist organisations across the globe

Members of the European Group for the Study of Deviance and Social Control (http://www.europeangroup.org/) and the Centre for the Study of Crime, Criminalisation and Social Exclusion   (http://ljmu.ac.uk/HSS/CCSEResearchCentre.htm) would like to express their solidarity with the National Coalition of Anti-Deportation Campaigns (http://www.ncadc.org.uk/) in its struggle to end the inhuman and degrading treatment of people caught up in the asylum and immigration system in the UK. We call for an end to the criminalisation of refugees, migrants, and asylum seekers who are routinely denied access to fair justice and the right of sanctuary. We offer our solidarity to activists across the globe seeking to protect the rights and interests of migrants

APPENDIX 3:

The Centre for the Study of Crime, Criminalisation and Social Exclusion
In partnership with
The European Group for the Study of Deviance and Social Control

Sites of Confinement
22nd March 2013
Liverpool John Moores University
68 Hope Street, Liverpool

This day conference offers an opportunity to critically discuss increases n the uses of confinement and incarceration in relation to neoliberalism, globally as well as in the UK. With activists, researchers and academics working in prisons, detention centres and camps, it will consider the roles of social structures, power, and lived experience in relation to confinement. Importantly, this conference will consider increases in incarceration as a method of social control in areas of extreme deprivation, as well as with marginalised groups

This conference is free to attend, but limited to 80 participants. Please book in advance. As this is a free event, lunch will not be provided. However, refreshments will be available throughout the day.

The Centre for the Study of Crime, Criminalisation and Social Exclusion
Liverpool John Moores University
www.ljmu.ac.uk/HSS/CCSEResearchCentre.htm

Conference Schedule:

9am: Conference Registration
9.20am: Victoria Canning
Welcome and Outline

Section One: Problematising Confinement
9.30am: Emma Bell
The Confines of Neoliberalism
10am: Vickie Cooper
Semi-Penal Hostels and Networks of Punishment in the Community
10.30am: Andrew Jefferson
Confinement and Subjectivity: sites, embodied practices and entangled encounters

11am: Break and Refreshments

Section Two: Detention, Asylum and the State
11.30am: Monish Bhatia
Creating and Managing 'Mad', 'Bad' and 'Dangerous': The role of Asylum Control Industry
12pm: Roundtable: Asylum and Detention
Supporting Asylum Seekers at 'Revive'
Eloise Cockcroft and **'Revive'** service users will informally discuss the challenges
faced by people seeking asylum in terms of increased criminalisation,
detention and incarceration

1.30pm: Lunch break

Section Three: Where from Here?
2.30pm: David Scott
Escape Routes: Exit Strategies from Global Hyper-incarceration
3pm: Joe Sim
Exploring 'the edges of what is possible': Abolitionist Activism and Neoliberal Austerity
3.30pm: Launch
*European Group for the Study of Deviance and Social Control:
Prisons and Punishment Working Group*

3.45pm: Questions, Comments and Open Discussion

To book a place, please register here: http://confinement.eventbrite.com/#
For more information please contact Dr. Victoria Canning, e: v.canning@ljmu.ac.uk
The Centre for the Study of Crime, Criminalisation and Social Exclusion
Liverpool John Moores University

Also published by the European Group for the
Study of Deviance and Social Control

Beyond Criminal Justice
An Anthology of Abolitionist Papers

Edited by
J.M. Moore, Bill Rolston, David Scott and Mike Tomlinson

2014, 282 pages, £12.99

Beyond Criminal Justice presents a vision of a future without brutal, authoritarian and repressive penal regimes. Many of the papers brought together here have been unavailable for more than two decades. Their republication indicates not only their continuing theoretical importance to abolitionist studies but also how they provide important insights into the nature and legitimacy of criminal processes in the here and now. Contributors highlight the human consequences of the harms of imprisonment, evidencing the hurt, injury and damage of penal incarceration across a number of different countries in Europe. Focusing on penal power and prisoner contestation to such power, the moral and political crises of imprisonment are laid bare.

The contributors to *Beyond Criminal Justice* explore the urgent need for a coherent, rational and morally and politically sophisticated theoretical basis for penal abolitionism. Advocating a utopian imagination and at the same time practical solutions already implemented in countries around Europe - alongside grappling with controversial debates such as abolitionist responses to rape and sexual violence - the book steps outside of common sense assumptions regarding 'crime', punishment and 'criminal justice'. *Beyond Criminal Justice* will be of interest to students of criminology, zemiology, sociology, penology and critical legal studies as well as anyone interested in rethinking the problem of 'crime' and challenging the logic of the penal rationale.

CPSIA information can be obtained
at www.ICGtesting.com
Printed in the USA
LVOW07s1719210917
549566LV00010B/943/P